CW00420696

ADVANCE
TO GO

ADVANCE TO GO

"Win your financial freedom through property investment"

Samuel Oliver

Contents

Prologue

I had to make the offer without knowing if I could get planning permission. Chris was waiting on the call for an answer, what would my final offer be?

It was the spring of 2012 and I had just turned 22, the little one bedroom apartment that I had seen in the South Side of Edinburgh was on the market for £95,000. It was tiny, and in desperate need of renovation. It was also the only property that I had seen which was within my merger millennial budget.

The estate agent had set a closing date for high noon and the solicitor I had chosen to represent me, Chris, was waiting for my best and final offer. Aside from the low price, what had excited me about this property was the abandoned basement. If I could buy the property and get planning permission it would be possible to double the floor area and turn this cramped one bedroom property into a comfy two bedroom maisonette. With planning permission this property would be my own little gold mine, otherwise it was not going to make a great investment.

"Look Chris, £82,000 is as I high as I can go". I waited for his answer.

"I don't think it's going to be enough, that is £13,000 below asking and they've got other people interested". Chris explained.

"If I went higher, I wouldn't have any budget left for renovation and I don't even know if I can get planning permission, I'm sorry Chris this is the best I can do." I said.

"Okay I'll let you know as soon as I hear the outcome." Chris ended the call.

I spent the day anxiously waiting to find out if I had just bought my first ever property. Finally the call came. I could tell from Chris's tone that the news was bad. He explained that there had been a significantly higher offer, well over £100,000. My spark of youthful, naive excitement was dimmed.

In the 21st century getting on the property ladder seems akin to a mythical goal. After losing out to someone with a bigger budget I felt pretty depressed. In the preceding months every property I saw for sale was significantly over what I could afford. I was starting to think that I just didn't have enough money to make it. That was when I got a notification on my phone, one new email, from Chris.

Like all of his emails it was short and to the point:

"Hi Sam,

The sale has fallen through and the vendor urgently needs to complete, they will accept your previous offer of £82,000. Can you proceed?"

It was this stroke of luck that got my foot firmly on the property ladder. Without being aware of it, age 22, I started on the path to financial freedom. As the years go by, I've realised how fortunate I was to start investing in property from a young age. I am ever grateful for my good fortune and I hope that reading this book will bring you a little luck too.

Financial Freedom

I wrote this book to share what I've learned about property investment. Writing has helped me better understand the strategies that I've developed unintentionally over the years. By reading this book you will learn strategies that will liberate you from everyday economic worries and put you on the express path to your financial freedom.

To get started we need a common understanding of property investment terminology. This book focuses on 'Buy To Let' buying a property that you will rent to tenants. Properties make money in two ways, firstly by going up in value over time and secondly from rental income.

You've seen a property for sale at £230,000. You take out a mortgage from your bank and buy it. The person you buy it from is called 'the vendor'. The cash that you've had to spend is known as capital deployed. While you have spent money, theoretically you have not lost any money. In a healthy property market you could at any time sell the property to someone else for £230,000, and get your money back.

If the property market is rising, then you benefit from your property becoming worth more. House prices in the UK have grown by 54% during the last decade 2010-2020 according to Zoopla. That means if you had bought your investment property for £230,000 in 2010 it would then be worth £354,200 in 2020. If you had sold you would have made a £124,200 profit. This increase in the value of your property is called capital appreciation.

The property market can fall in value, for instance in some areas of the UK prices fell by 20% during the 'Credit Crunch' of 2007. If you bought your property in 2006 for £230,000 then tried to sell it in 2008 you may have only been able to sell for £184,000 a loss of £46,000. This is capital depreciation.

While you can't predict the future, if you hold your property investments for the long term it is very likely that you will make a large capital appreciation. If you're worried about buying at a high price and selling at a loss, then head over to YouTube and spend 30 minutes watching Ray Dalio's excellent video called 'The Economy' which neatly explains economic cycles.

The second way that your property investment will make money is through rental income. For example you've bought your property for £230,000 and you rent it out for £1,900 per month. Your annual rental income is £22,800. This means your property has a rental yield of 9.9% per year.

As a property investor you're interested in three percentages:

1. Capital appreciation (how much your property has gone up in value).

2. Rental yield (how much your property is earning for you each year).

3. Mortgage rate (how much you are charged for borrowing money).

To win your financial freedom, you need the capital value appreciation and rental income to be higher than your annual expenditure on maintenance, management and mortgage interest. In the following chapters you'll learn how.

The Secret of Now

The first secret I'm going to share with you is about understanding time. Patience is one of the keys to building your financial freedom and your wealth. Once you understand this, you'll also see the urgency of getting started today because making a lot of money takes time and the longer you delay starting, the longer you'll have to wait to succeed.

You've worked hard for many years and you've managed to save up £23,000. This money is safely parked in your bank account, and your bank is paying you a 'whopping' 1% interest rate. So at the end of the year in your bank account you'll have £23,230. Great you've got an extra £230! If you leave that money in the bank slowly growing for 10 years you'll have £25,406. Great news, over 10 years you've got an extra £2,406.

Imagine that instead of leaving that £23,000 in the bank, back in 2010 you used it as the deposit to buy a £230,000 house, the value of the house rose by 54% and over the 10 years you've earned £124,200. That's a whole lot better than the £2,406 you would have made by leaving money in the bank…

In both scenarios you're benefiting from compound interest, your money grows over time. Leave that £23,000 in the bank at 1% interest and after 354 years you'll have £1,000,000.

With a property market that grows at 5.4% annually if you buy that investment property for £230,000 then after 29 years it will be worth £1,043,120.

As Albert Einstein said, "Compound interest is the most powerful force in the universe. It is the 8th wonder of the world. He who understands it, earns it; he who doesn't, pays it."

Compound interest is a force at your disposal, a tool for you to wield in the financial battle to earn your freedom. No matter how much money you start with, or how high an interest percentage you earn, the sooner you get started the faster you'll be free.

There is of course a catch to this all powerful universal force... while time may be infinite, human lifespan isn't. We don't have hundreds of years to leave money in an account earning interest, so how can we speed the process up, how can we make wealth faster, how can we hack the system?

The Secret of Leverage

Well there are two ways to change the mathematical formula and make compound interest work in your favour. These are the two most vital secrets of property investment, the two levers that you need to pull to reach your freedom. You want to earn the highest interest rate possible and to be earning interest on the biggest possible amount.

So let's imagine you can pull the interest rate lever. You put £23,000 in your savings account and the bank manager says to you, "Because you're special I'm going to give you an interest rate of 10% each year!" Brilliant news… This has changed EVERYTHING. If you leave your money in the bank for 10 years the interest rate compounds and your nest egg will grow to £59,656.

Wouldn't it be useful if the bank manager went a little crazy and said to you "Since you are such a loyal customer, such an upstanding member of the public, we're going to give you a 25% interest rate". Now we are really talking. Leave your money in the bank for 10 years while the interest rate compounds and your nest egg will grow to £214,204.

So how can you earn these crazy high yields on your money? You need to go into debt.

Debt is good, debt is opportunity, debt is power. Society likes to keep you believing that debt is a dirty word, you should never get into debt. I urge you to challenge this belief because it's wrong. Property millionaires know the truth, debt is a good thing, they have used the power of debt and compound interest to escape the norms of society and win their financial freedom and you can too.

Debt is good because you can earn interest on it.

This is an incredibly important concept to understand, please hear me out, open your mind and learn this secret. If you are not able to get comfortable with debt then property investment is not for you.

You've borrowed £210,000 from the bank and you've agreed to pay 3% interest on it. You've invested in a property that pays you 10% a year. What is the interest rate you earn on the bank's money? Bingo 10%-3%= 7%. This simple sum, this maths that a 4 year old child (or a gifted 3 year old) could do, is the secret to you making as much money as you want.

When you invest money at a higher return than you borrow it, you're making a profit on money that is not yours! In the investment world this is called arbitrage, in the property world it's called leverage.

Understanding the secret of leverage works best with some examples.

Let's imagine that you've been saving for a very long time, and that you've saved up a total of £230,000. With this money you've bought an investment property. You've let this property out and each year you get paid £23,000. What is your yield? Yield is the return on investment as a percentage. The rental income £23,000 divided by the amount invested £230,000 which gives a 10% yield.

Congratulations you've just worked out the 'Gross Yield' of an investment property! Look at you go, you're getting familiar with the technical jargon already. Gross yield means we've not taken off any of the costs associated with running the property or taxes. We'll keep it simple and stick to gross yield for now, and later on we'll get more technical and discuss the joys of TAX!

So you've done a good job as you've managed to get a high yield of 10%; you've successfully pulled the first lever of property investment.

How could you make more money? How can you grow your wealth faster?

Rather than waiting until you have £230,000 to buy the property, you save up £20,000 and go to the bank and secure a loan at a good rate. You will be pulling the second lever; earning a profit on money you don't actually have.

You buy the same property for £230,000. As you only had £20,000 saved you borrow £210,000 from the bank at an interest rate of 3% per year. The annual rental is still £23,000 per year so the gross yield is still 10%.

Your return on your £20,000 is not 10%. You have used the secret of leverage to boost it.

Here's the maths. You put in £20,000 and the bank put in £210,000. Every year you have to pay the bank £6,300 in interest (£210,000 * 3%). The rental of the property brings in £23,000 per year. After deducting the cost of the interest, you are making £16,700 (£23,000 - £6,300). This means that your £20,000 is returning £16,700 per year! That is a return of 83%. (£16,700/£20,000*100). In the property investment world we call this the 'Geared Yield'.

You have played the leverage game, you borrowed £210,000 at 3% and invested it into an asset making 10% so you made a 7% return on money that you didn't have to save. You used your £20,000 in a way that earned you 83% interest per year.

Now you can see the power of DEBT, you can earn interest on 'savings' that you don't even have. The bank will lend you hundreds of thousands of pounds, millions even, and you can earn interest on. You're not going to have to wait 29 years to make £100,000,000. You are going to make it a lot faster than that.

You can see that by investing in a property that has a good rental return and by borrowing money from the bank at a sensible interest rate, it's possible to get an incredibly good return. There is of course a golden rule... always make sure your investment is returning more than you pay in interest rates.

Compound interest cuts both ways. If you've invested in a property returning 4% a year, and the bank changes interest rates to 6% all of a sudden you are paying 2%. You become the loser at the end of this equation, compound interest is no longer on your side, it has switched allegiance. This is one of the only times that debt is dangerous to you. We'll review some of the other ways you can protect yourself from risks involved in debt later in the book . In a couple of chapters you'll become very familiar with the word cashflow…

As a property investor you have two jobs, and only two jobs. The first, invest in properties that give you the HIGHEST possible return (capital appreciation, and rental return). The second, invest as MUCH as you can. Let's get really comfortable with what I mean here, I mean BORROW as much as you can (with as low interest rates as you can). Now that you understand what you need to do, and why it makes financial sense, let's get practical and look at how you can do it.

The Deposit Challenge

Every snowman starts off as a tiny snowball. When buying a property, the deposit is your snowball. If you're buying a property using a mortgage, the deposit is the amount of money you must have saved while the remainder of the property purchase price is lent to you by a lender, usually a bank or a building society.

The biggest barrier to property investment is access to a deposit. Once you've saved, begged and borrowed enough money to have a deposit on a property, then you can go to the lender to get a mortgage. With your financing arranged you can search for and buy a property. Last but not least you're going to rent the property, collect your income and become financially free.

That's it, your plan in one single paragraph. Starting out on this journey can be hard, it can be daunting. I've been there, and I've made all the mistakes. I'm going to go through the whole process so that you don't make any mistakes. Every stage is connected, and not in a simple linear way. How can you know how much to pay for a property if you don't know how much the rent will be? How can you know how much of a deposit you need to have if you don't know how much the lender will lend you, or how much your investment property will cost?

Make it to the end of this book and you'll learn more property secrets. You don't need as much money as you think, the bank will lend you more than you think and you can get the rental income to be higher than you think. In the coming chapters I am going to share with you all of the tips, tricks and truths that other people won't.

The deposit is a catch 22, it's hard to get excited and motivated about your deposit if you don't know how big it needs to be. So we're going to have to jump ahead a little. The lender will decide how much money to lend you based on three main factors. How much money you earn, what the rental income of the property will be and what the property is worth.

To calculate the deposit that you'll need to save we must first know the cost of the property. The lender will calculate your deposit based on a ratio called the loan to value ratio. Often abbreviated to LTV%. Before agreeing to lend money the lender will send out a surveyor that they trust to value the property. They will then lend you money based on that valuation.

Lenders will usually offer a LTV of up to 95%. This means that if you want to buy a property that costs £100,000 and the lender offers you a 95% LTV they will lend you £95,000 and you will have to have £5,000 as the deposit.

We will talk a lot about mortgages later, but as a rough rule of thumb you should use a 80% LTV in order to calculate the deposit that you will need.

So if you're buying a £100,000 property with a 80% LTV mortgage you'll need a £20,000 deposit.

If you're buying a £230,000 property with a 80% LTV what deposit will you need?

£230,000 * 20% = £46,000.

Getting a deposit together is the HARDEST part of property investment and is the biggest barrier to most people. To get started with your first property investment and to make the deposit as small as possible you'll want to try and get a high LTV from the lender, and buy a cheap property.

Let's assume your first property costs £180,000 at a 80% LTV. You're going to need to save £36,000...

How are you going to do that? Have you got any thoughts? If you're in the excellent position of having the deposit that you need, feel free to skip this chapter. If you feel that getting a deposit together is going to be difficult or downright impossible, read on...

First things first, how much money have you got? £4,700? Great, that is a good start. Have you got some extra cash sloshing around in your current account, that you can avoid spending. Let's say that you can transfer £300 from your current account into your savings account.

Marvellous, you're up to a nice round £5,000 but you are still £31,000 away from what you need...

Once you've checked through all your various bank accounts and moved everything into one place it's time to look at your other assets. It's liquidation time. Do you hold any stocks and shares, or any bonds? Sell them. I'm serious. Sell them. You, or your parents, or your financial advisor (definitely your financial advisor) will need some serious convincing on this. You might need to revisit this stage, when you've picked a property, a mortgage and you know what your rental yield is going to be. Then you can clearly argue why investing your money in property is going to return better than any other investment asset.

The only time that you don't want to liquidate investments is if there has just been a 10 year cyclical economic crash, wait for prices to recover in value before selling. (watch that 30 minute video called The Economy, by Ray Dalio if you want more context here) Some investments will also have penalties if you cash them in before a certain date. Watch out for this.

I don't want to get into a huge discussion about investing in stocks VS investing in property. So I will keep my argument to a minimum, I don't own any stocks, I don't own any bonds, I don't have any crypto currency, I don't have a pension. All of my assets are in property, where they are safe, produce a great return and I understand exactly what my money is doing and how it's helping people. (I own shares in my own LTD companies, but not any publicly traded companies).

Okay let's get back to finding you that extra £31,000 that you need to buy your first investment property. The liquidation must continue. You've sold off your financial assets, now it's time to sell your real world assets. Once again I'm completely serious. Shoes, clothes, jewellery, cars, furniture, anything that can help you pull together some money.

Selling your stuff is a good exercise, for a few reasons: firstly, it's going to be motivating when you make your first £100, then £500 and then you've sold £1,000 of stuff and you realise that you've now got £6,000 in the bank and you've only got £30,000 to go. The second reason why selling stuff is good, you're going to realise how little you get back for things. That sofa that you bought in the high street shop for £800 only sold for £80. This painful lesson is going to be super important in your next step, cutting back on your spending. The next time you buy a sofa you're going to look for a nice second hand one for £80 before you buy a brand new one and overpay by £720!

Now... I can hear what you're thinking. I like nice stuff. I deserve new stuff. I want my things to be pristine. Great. Good for you. You don't deserve it yet. I'm serious. You've not earned the good things yet. If you keep spending and don't build up enough money to buy your first investment property you will forever stay in the avocado covered millennial wealth trap. You'll never have financial freedom. You will always be spending money on credit and having compound interest working against you. Do you want the most powerful force in the universe working against you?

If you can't afford to buy your first investment property, you can't afford designer clothes, or an expensive holiday. I can not stress this enough. Cut back on your spending, pay for those things out of your rental income when you've earned it.

Now if you want to spend your life as a wage slave. Someone who must work to live. Then put this book down. Throw it away. You don't have what it takes to reach financial freedom. You'll always be reliant on a job and the more money you earn, the more you'll spend. You'll never be free to do as you wish, knowing you've built security and stability in your life from your savvy financial decisions. If you want this future, you're going to have to sacrifice. You're going to have to cut down on your spending. The more you want financial freedom the faster it's going to happen for you.

How much can you save per month? £100, perhaps £500? It's not enough. You're going to have to get radical, stop eating out at restaurants, stop getting your Starbucks coffee every day, and cancel holiday plans abroad. Let's get to a more ambitious savings target, you're going to save half of your income each month, for argument's sake £1,000 per month.

So you've got £6,000 in the bank from pooling your cash together and from selling things you don't really need and never use. You're now cutting back on your spending and you're saving £1,000 per month. It's going to take you 30 months to save up all the way to £36,000. Ouch 30 months that is two and half years with no holidays and no restaurant visits. It's a long time. But, it's not that long. There is also one last strategy that you can use.

Over the past few months you've told your friends and family that you can't go on holiday, they've seen you going to the post office to send all the things that you've been selling online. You've been telling them about your house hunt, about how excited you are to buy your first investment property. There is a sparkle in your eyes, there is a buzz about you. There is excitement. Your people know that you are on a mission. They know that you're serious, you're dedicated, you're going to put in the time, that you are going to make this happen.

Your people will want to help you.

This is one of the keys to getting started in property, some call it 'the bank of mum and dad', but it's much more than that. It also has to be your last step to getting your deposit together.

You've got to show people that you are committed to reaching your goal and that you are making sacrifices to your wardrobe and your lifestyle in order to make this happen. People will respect you when they see how much effort and energy you're putting in, they will want to support you.

Doing property alone is hard, £36,000 is a lot of money and two and a half years is a lot of time to sacrifice your lifestyle. Shrug off your dignity and ask your people for help.

When I bought my first property I borrowed money from EVERYONE, my mum, dad, brothers, sister. My 86 year old granny even gave a stack of crumpled, dusty, near antique £20 notes that had been squirrelled away somewhere.

Just as you had diligently built up a few thousand pounds in your savings account your close network will also have some cash available, sitting there, earning negligible interest in a bank account. Or they will have a second car sitting in the garage that they can't be bothered selling.

You are the fire-starter, the motivated one, the person on a mission. Your family network WILL want to support you, so crowd-fund.

Perhaps the bank of Mum and Dad can lend you an extra £8,000. Each aunty, uncle, cousin, brother, sister can lend you £200 - £500. A lot of money but not such a big amount that they won't have it, or they won't feel comfortable lending it to you. Especially when they see all the lifestyle changes you've made and all the sacrifices you've taken to make this deposit happen. Also, break the taboos and ask your grandparents and parents about inheritance, can you have some early? Not to squander but to invest. Are there some stocks and bonds in your name that you don't know about? Your family will be impressed that you're taking your financial future seriously and they will want to support you on your mission.

Share your story with your family, tell them why you're excited, show them all your research into the property you want to buy, and don't be nervous or shy about putting their money to work.

It is SUPER important to keep a ledger of who has lent you money, and how long it will take you to pay them back. Really you want to tell people that you need the money for a year or two. In reality when someone has lent you £600 for two years, they don't miss it, and it's likely to be okay if you take five or six years to pay them back. The point is you're not asking for a gift, you will pay them back, you just need their help in accomplishing your goal.

So let's assume that you managed to squeeze £14,000 from the extended bank of mum and dad... You've gone from thinking that owning a property is something that is completely out of your reach, you've gone from thinking the few thousands of pounds in your bank account will never be enough to get a deposit to having £20,000 of the £36,000 you need.

You're well over half way, you're only short £16,000 that is 16 months of saving. If you push yourself even harder, you could get enough money before the end of the year! You're so close! Stay focused, stay saving and check your bank balance to see how far away you are from your goal, this is exciting!

Keep plugging away at saving money, and don't worry if you've got a year until you are ready, because it can take a long time to find the right investment property. You're a patient investor playing the long game, you're not in a rush!

It's Your Bank

Now that you're excited about getting into debt and making a profit on the bank's money, it's time to get a mortgage. So what is a mortgage? It's a loan for buying property, the lender will give you a sum of money and they will expect you to pay it back over time with interest. That's it!

In this chapter we'll talk about all the different ways that lender dress-up mortgages. We'll go through the difference between interest-only & capital repayment and fixed rates and & tracker rates.Together we'll strip away all the layers to help you pick the most profitable option.

If you're buying your first property it's most likely that you will apply for a mortgage in your own name, however if you're planning on buying many properties you might start a limited business. We'll talk about the pros and cons of starting a property company in a later chapter. If you do go down that route you'll need to apply for a company mortgage. This decision doesn't affect how mortgages work but it's important to know that not all lenders will lend to companies.

The lender doesn't want to lose money so they are going to make you jump through hoops to reduce their risk before handing you over hundreds of thousands of pounds. Once a lender has decided to lend to you, they will give you a 'mortgage in principle' which means that they will lend you a set amount of money, but the offer is not confirmed until they have sent a surveyor to value the property. Lenders will set a limit on how much money they will lend to you. As a rough rule they will lend four times your income, so if you earn £50,000 a year they will lend you up to £200,000.

Lenders can be aggressive businesses, they want to make money from you, and they compete hard against each other. The fundamentals of a mortgage are pretty simple, only one thing matters, how much interest you have to pay each year. As all banks are selling the same thing, they have made it as confusing and complicated as possible to tell the differences between the mortgages that they offer.

In truth, lenders do not have your best interest at heart, you are going to have to outsmart them. You're driven, motivated and you're going to make their money work for you.

So let's delve into the dark art of mortgages together, I'll try to make this as fun as possible for you, I promise!

There are two different types of mortgage: interest-only and capital repayment.

You've gone for an interest-only mortgage. The lender has agreed to lend you £100,000 for 10 years at an interest rate of 5%. This means that every year you have to pay the lender £5,000. At the end of the 10 years, you will still owe the lender £100,000 you will either have to sell the property to pay them back, have £100,000 cash laying about, or, what normally happens, you'll get another mortgage either from them or another lender. Over the 10 years of the mortgage you'll have paid the lender £50,000 in interest and you will still owe them £100,000. Don't be disheartened by this, remember that you'll have made way over £50,000 in rental income over the 10 years, and the value of the property will likely be a lot higher too!

The second type of mortgage is a capital repayment mortgage. Let's go with the same example, you borrow £100,000 for 10 years at a 5% interest rate. Every month the lender wants you to pay the interest on the loan, and also part of the capital that you borrowed, the £100,000. So every year they want you to pay back £12,732. You're paying a lot more each year than you are on the interest only loan, but at the end of the 10 years you'll have paid the lender, £127,320. You'll have paid them £100,000 back, and a total of £27,320 in interest.

So which type of mortgage do you prefer? Interest only, or capital repayment?

Most people think that debt is bad, and they want to make sure that they are repaying it every year. Thus the common belief is that you should get a repayment mortgage so you pay off your debts. Why pay £50,000 in interest to the bank when you could pay £27,320. Surely it's better to pay less interest over all by choosing a repayment mortgage. No. As we went through in the previous chapter, leverage is good. If you have bought an investment property returning 9% a year and you're paying the bank 5% year interest on the £100,000 money they have lent you, then you are making 4% interest a year on a £100,000 cash that isn't yours! Yes over 10 years you pay the bank £50,000 in interest but you make £40,000 profit on their capital.

One of the main reasons that property investors choose interest-only mortgages is that it frees up their cash flow. Instead of paying back the loan, they have more money every month accruing in their account. This money can then be used as a deposit to buy another property growing your wealth and income even faster.

Remember the second law of property investment, you always want to have as much money as possible in your control, so that you can make interest on it. You want to get as much money as you can from the bank, and not pay them back anything, other than the interest! Stay in debt, debt is good.

It's not always possible to get an interest-only mortgage, the lender is not your friend and doesn't want to risk its money. They often increase the interest rates on interest-only mortgages. You may be presented with two options. A repayment mortgage at 5% interest, or an interest-only mortgage at 7% interest. To make comparing mortgage choices easier, I've created a mortgage comparison calculator on my website.

The next variable in your mortgage selection is interest rates. Lenders will offer you the choice between a fixed interest rate or a tracker interest rate and they will make these offers over specific time periods.

A fixed interest rate means that you'll know exactly what percentage interest you'll pay over a certain time period, for example the lender might offer you a 5% interest rate for 3 years. A tracker rate is a fixed amount above the Bank of England's base rate. For instance 3% above the base rate. So when the base rate is 0.75% you pay 3.75% if the base rate goes up to 6% then you pay 9%. Tracker interest rates follow the base rate set by a central authority, in the UK it's the bank of England base rate or LIBOR (The London Inter-Bank Offered Rate) while in the US it's set by the Federal Reserve.

If lenders were your friends they would give you the very best rate possible. They are not 'your friend', they want to make a profit from you. Lenders want to confuse you, so they offer lots of different mortgage combinations. A tracker rate, a 2 year fixed rate, a 5 year fixed rate, all at different interest rates. So how do you know which to pick?

Now is the time for you to become an economist and predict the future of the Bank of England base rate... The gamble that you have to choose when selecting between a tracker mortgage or a fixed rate mortgage is deciding what you think will happen to the base rate. For instance if choice A is the fixed rate mortgage at 5% for three years versus choice B, the tracker at 1.5% above base, currently 0.75, then B at 2.25% looks a lot better A at 5%.

However if something CRAZY happened and the bank of England put the base interest rate up to 7.5% next year. Then the tracker mortgage would be 8% while the fixed mortgage would be 5%. A clear winner in the other direction.

It's impossible to predict the future, so it's impossible to know exactly what the best option is. However let me pitch a theory to you. Who knows more about interest rates, you or the lender? My guess is the lender. The lender is likely to better predict the future of interest rates than you are. This means they will always offer fixed rate loans that they think will be profitable for them, they always expect the fixed rate loan will make them more money than the tracker. A lender wouldn't offer you a five year fixed rate at 3% if it believed that the base rate would go up to 5% next year, because then the lender would be losing out, and the lender always wants to win. Remember... lenders have warehouses of analysts and computers trying to predict the future, they are not messing around when it comes to making money from you.

If there is a really good deal, say a 10 year fixed rate at 3% or a tracker at 1.25% above base, so that is 2%, (=1.25% + 0.75%),then you might want to assume that interest rates will go up more than 1% in the next 10 years and take the fixed rate. I'd still take the tracker, because if it takes 5 years for the interest rates to change, and after 5 years the tracker mortgage including base rate rises to 4% you'll have paid;- 2% for 5 years and 4% for 5 years, so that is 3% over all, the same as the fixed rate. The bank is always trying to confuse and tempt you with offers, and deals. Take your time, research interest rate predictions online, and decide what you want to do. If in doubt, take the tracker.

Okay, so there are interest-only mortgages and repayment mortgages, there are fixed interest rates and tracker interest rates. Not so complicated right?

Ha, the lenders are NOT done trying to confuse you yet. They are going to throw in ANOTHER hurdle. The set-up fee, they will also call this fee different names, once again to confuse you. Sometimes it will be called a booking fee, sometimes a set-up fee, sometimes a 'because we can fee'. This is a layer of complication we could do without, but we will cut through it together. Set-up fees normally come in two different forms. Either a fixed amount for instance £1,999, or a percentage of the money borrowed e.g. 1.5% set-up fee on the amount borrowed. So for example you're borrowing £100,000 and you have those two fee options. Either you can pay £1999 or 1.5% of £100,000 so £1,500. In that example it's better to take the percentage fee. However if you were borrowing £200,000 it's different. You could either pay £1999 or 1.5% of £200,000 which is. £3,000. So in that example you'd be better to-pay the fixed fee.

See how sneaky they are!

Now, we're going to add another variable into the mortgage mix. How much money you want to borrow. We touched on this earlier, when calculating your deposit. It's the Loan to Value LTV. Let's go big in this example. You're buying a £1m property. The bank gives you a 95% LTV so they will lend you £950,000 and you need to have £50,000 as a deposit.

Lenders will combine all of these variables into 'Products' for you to choose from. So let's run through what those options look like.

1. Interest Only or Capital Repayment
2. Fixed interest rate for a number of years, V.S. tracking the central bank base rate.
3. Set Up Fees varying from none, to a set amount, to a percentage.
4. LTV ratio.

Those are the four sets of variables that the lender can rearrange and bewilder you with. On the lender's website, looking through the mortgage list, you might see 20 to 120 different mortgage options, which will regularly change. The best way to really understand this, is to create a spreadsheet and write out some examples using their offers, or use my mortgage comparison calculator www.advancetogo.com/mortgage-comparison. Put in the value of the property you want to buy, and look at the actual costs over time of each mortgage. Then decide if you think the bank of England base rate is going to change.

Now you understand how mortgages work, congratulations! You probably understand them better than the bank employee who will try to sell you one. Applying for a mortgage can be quite intimidating, as lenders are often huge multinational corporations that turn over more money a year than some small nations. Don't be intimidated by them, I am going to let you in on another property investment secret. Even the biggest bank is no different from a fruit and vegetable stall at your local farmers' market. I am serious! It's just a business trying to sell you, the consumer, a product. It's not doing you some huge favour, you are the customer and you are doing the lender a favour. Do not forget that you have power. With power comes leverage. You've got to haggle with the lender.

What? Haggle with the lender. That's right. If you want to really crush it as a property investor, and you want to build a comfortable lifestyle of nice holidays, then you know that every £500 is important and anywhere that you can make a saving gets you to your deposit faster and your financial freedom faster. You can haggle with lenders if you speak to the right person, someone senior who has the authority to give you a discount. It is possible to haggle on the interest rate, but you're more likely to be able to haggle on the set-up fee.

Make it perfectly clear to the senior mortgage advisor or bank manager that you know over the 20 years of the mortgage you'll be paying them tens of thousands of pounds in interest payments. Make it perfectly clear that you have other options, and you will work with one of their competitors if they do not remove the set up fee. You should employ this tactic at the end of the process, not the start. Jump through all of the lender's v eligibility hoops and criteria, then just before you sign the deal and give them the victory they want, get rid of that set-up fee. Remember the bank manager has performance targets and they don't want to lose your business, you have the power here. Also don't be scared of actually walking away and working with another lender. If you're saving £1000 a month towards your deposit by missing all your luxuries, then saving £1999 on the set up fee is a big deal, you can be patient and speak to a number of mortgage providers. They are lucky to have you, you are awesome.

Alas we've only gone through half the battle with mortgages. If you need to take a break and have a cup of coffee, I understand. I've had two coffees just writing this! Don't go and spend £12.50 on avocado toast on rye bread though, that's not okay. Even if it does come with chilli flakes and saffron sprinkles.

Mortgage Ethics

Now that you've been armed with a framework for comparing mortgages you can figure out which is the best choice for you. Alas your work isn't over, once you've chosen a mortgage you then have to convince the lender that they can trust you with hundreds of thousands of pounds.

To understand this, we need to explore the confusing world of mortgages a little bit further as there are yet more variables at play. There are two different types of mortgages: a home mortgage, or a buy-to-let mortgage. So what's the difference? A home mortgage is when you borrow money to buy a property you will live in, not to rent out. A buy to let mortgage is when you're buying the property specifically to rent out to tenants.

The lender wants to know how credit worthy you are. They want to know the maximum amount of money they can lend you with the lowest amount of risk. To work this out they will ask you a lot of questions. The main one is simple, how much money a year do you make?

For example if you earn £20,000 a year, the lender will usually let you borrow 4 or 5 times your salary. In this example they would lend you £80,000 to £100,000.

The lender also wants to know that you can afford to pay them back each month, so they will ask you in detail how much money you spend. They will look at the amount of money you make each month and the amount of money you spend each month and they will decide if they think you will be able to afford the mortgage. (This is where lenders got into a lot of trouble in the financial crisis, they lent loads of money to people who couldn't afford to pay it back, so they have become quite strict on this now).

Lenders will usually want to see three months' bank statements, payslips and an employment contract as proof of your income. They will also want to know if your contract is permanent or if there is a chance you might lose your income.

When you're buying a property to let, the bank will look at it a little differently. They will usually want the rental from the property to be 150% of the monthly repayments. What does this mean? If the monthly mortgage repayments work out as £1,000 a month, the bank will want the rent to be at least £1,500 a month. This way they feel comfortable that with the extra money coming in, you'll always be able to pay them.

These are the basic ways that the bank will decide how much money to lend you. They will also look at your credit history, to see if you've messed up in the past. If you've been to court over money, or have been declared bankrupt, it will be harder for you to borrow money.

There are more pros for a home mortgage than a buy to let mortgage. Home mortgages will nearly always have a better interest rate and have a higher LTV, meaning you can borrow more towards the cost of the house. Buy to let mortgages have higher interest rates, and you will not be able to borrow as much, because lenders see them as higher risk loans.

The pro's for buy to let mortgages can often come if you have a very low personal income, the lender will look at the rental income not your personal income in order to decide if they want to lend the money, however they will often only do this if you already own your own home as they want to make sure you have assets they can hold as security if you can't pay them back.

This is the biggest problem with a buy to let mortgage, the lender will usually not give you one unless you already own your own home.

This is a real problem. A really, really big problem and it's going to lead to the darkest truth that you won't learn in ANY OTHER PROPERTY INVESTMENT BOOK.

Many property investors buy their first property in their own name using a personal mortgage, and then rent it out later. Let's discuss this in more detail to see just how ethical this is, and to see if it is the strategy you should take.

Please note, I'm not suggesting you break any contracts by fraudulently applying for a personal mortgage that you then rent out as a buy to let. If you take out a personal mortgage and then later rent it out as a buy to let at a later date this is allowed in most mortgage contracts as long as you notify the lender. I am suggesting you may enter into a contract knowing you will have to change it at a later date. Please be patient and read on to understand why this strategy is moral and legal. You've probably bought this book because you don't want to be a wage slave for the rest of your life. Escaping the norm, and earning your financial freedom requires strategic thinking.

So, how does this work? 100% go into the mortgage process hand on heart wanting to buy the property so you can live there. This is a key part of my philosophy and we'll talk more about it later when discussing how to choose an investment property. I've never bought a house that I wouldn't want to live in. If I fell on hard times I'd be very happy to live in any of my rental properties. My rental properties are much nicer than many places that I have rented to live in.

Go into the mortgage meeting 'planning' to buy your first house and be comfortable that you could live there if you wanted. This is your mind set for all of the mortgage meetings with the lender.

In the mortgage contract there will normally be the following clauses written in some overly technical legal jargon but meaning.

1. It's okay to let the property out while you still live there. So for instance if you buy a two bedroom flat and you live in one room and rent out the other, the lender doesn't care and you're not breaching the contract.

2. It's okay to let out the whole property. Lenders know that plans change over the years, perhaps you have to move abroad for a job, perhaps you move in with a partner. If you want to let the whole property the lender is usually okay with that. Most lenders have a 'Permission to let' form and will grant you permission to let the property for 12 months and then ask you to re-apply if you want to let the property out again.

What the contract won't say is that if you let the property out and don't tell the lender they will be very disappointed, they won't send you a Christmas card and Santa will bring you a big bag of coal. I'm serious, if you rent the property out, but you pay the mortgage every month, does the lender care?

Hopefully you're feeling a lot more comfortable about applying the strategy of using a home owner mortgage and then changing to letting the property out, but if you're not, let me share with you another truth about what lenders do, that may realign the centre of your moral compass.

When you take out a mortgage, even a tracker mortgage it will be valid for a set number of years. For instance a 5 year tracker. At the end of those 5 years the lender will change your mortgage interest rate to its 'standard variable tracker' aka "screw-you-over-rate', which is usually two or three times more than your initial interest rate.

The lender knows you need the mortgage for 20 or more years, the 5 year deal they give you is called the 'teaser' rate. They know that in five years time you'll have forgotten that they will move you onto a more expensive mortgage rate, they will quietly sit back and let you overpay them.

I learned this the hard way, with my first mortgage at the end of the teaser they moved me to a more expensive rate, I didn't notice and I was overpaying them. When I finally got my act in gear and remortgaged, I learned that I had pointlessly been over-paying my bank by £1,780 a year for three years. OUCH. I was scrimping and saving money for my next property, and I'd foolishly been over-paying the bank by thousands. It hurt. It was a reminder that my bank really didn't have my best interest at heart and simply wanted to make a profit from me.

Lenders won't play nice. I don't see why you should either. Go down the personal mortgage route and follow the contract TO THE LETTER. Once you've bought the property then notify the lender that your circumstances have changed and you need to let the property out. When the lender has gone through all of the hassle of assessing your credit worthiness, valuing the property, completing the legal paperwork and lending you the money, they don't want to take the mortgage away. This strategy doesn't break a single rule and will get you a bigger loan at a better interest rate. It's possible that the lender would not offer you a buy to let loan, so this may be your only option.

So practically where do you start to get a mortgage? The easiest step is to book a meeting with the mortgage advisor at your current bank. Your current bank has all of your account history, which makes it easy for them to check how much you earn and how much you spend. They also have your proof of ID and proof of address, so you've got a head-start on the administrative hoops you need to jump through in order to take out a mortgage.

Banks and building societies are the best places to arrange a mortgage. Do your research online, and compare as many mortgages as you can. There is also a sizable industry of mortgage brokers. The lenders pay the brokers for selling their mortgages. There can be a hidden conflict of interest here where the broker may recommend a mortgage for you based on how much they will be paid. Many brokers only work for a few lenders, if possible you want to work with a 'whole of market' broker, who has access to every single mortgage option in the UK so that you get the best deal.

Should you go direct or should you use a broker? It's a tricky question. The mortgage industry is so murky that some lenders will only let you apply through a mortgage broker, so by not using one you could miss out on a good rate. Do as much research online, and with your bank as you can. Then use a fee-free 'whole-of-market' broker.

So, to summarise this chapter on mortgages. The bank isn't your friend and will try to confuse you.Use the personal mortgage option and borrow as much as you can, as cheaply as possible. Take your time to do the maths and work out which mortgage is best for you. Remember everyone has hidden interests and is trying to make money from you. Don't let emotions or conformity pressure from your friends, family, or the lender cloud your judgement. Debt is your friend and compound interest is the most powerful force in the universe. A good spreadsheet and a few cups of coffee will always help you find the best financial option.

Life, Death & Taxes

It's inevitable that you're going to pay tax, but you may have some control over how much. In this chapter we will learn about tax planning. In most parts of the book there are very clear right and wrong answers. Tax is different. So much depends on your personal circumstances, tax law is regularly changed, and is geographically specific. This means you'll need to do your own research or speak to a tax advisor before making any decisions, this chapter is an outline guide only.

Simplistically you have two choices of tax structures. Either you can buy the property in your own name, or you can set up a limited company (Ltd.), sometimes you will hear this referred to as a SPV (Special Purpose Vehicle).

When you buy a property over £125,000 you have to pay land tax, the amount increases with the price of the property. There is another property tax called second homes tax. If you already own a property and you buy another one, the rate of tax you have to pay is significantly higher. When a LTD company buys a property it automatically has to pay the Second Home tax even if you don't own a property personally. Thus if you don't own any property it may be better to buy the first one in your own name.

Your personal tax rate has a big impact on the decision to buy as a company. The rental money that comes in from the property every year is classed by HMRC as unearned income. The amount of tax you have to pay on this income is decided by your tax band. If you have a high personal earned income, from your salary, then you will pay more tax on your rental income. For example, if you earn £20,000 a year from your salary and your property income is £10,000 a year, your tax band will be 20%. This means you will pay £2,000 of your rent in tax. Comparatively if you earn £110,000 a year from your salary and your property income is £10,000 then your tax band will be 40% and you'll pay £4,000 in tax. As you can see the more money you make in salary, the more tax you pay on rent. Buying as a LTD company can give you an advantage. You can take the money out of the company as a dividend, or through a pension plan, you still have to pay tax on the rent but depending on your circumstances there may be ways to pay less than buying as an individual.

Finally on the tax front we need to consider expenses. When buying a property in your own name you can't claim interest rate payments as an expense. Let's assume that you foolishly didn't read this book and you made a very bad property investment. Your property makes £10,000 a year in rental, but you borrowed money at an expensive interest rate so you have to pay the lender £10,000 in interest. As an individual you will still have to pay tax on the £10,000 rent even though you've not made a profit from renting out the property. If you are on that 40% tax band you'd have to pay £4,000 in tax and your property investment would be making you a loss. However if you'd set up this poor property investment as a LTD then HMRC would view the accounting differently. Your £10,000 income is balanced by a £10,000 expense, the interest payments to the lender, so you have no profit. Thus HMRC will charge you no tax. This is a significant advantage of buying as a LTD. It can change an investment from being loss making to being profitable.

Usually when you take out a mortgage in your own name the lender will charge you a lower interest rate than if you're buying a property through an LTD. Thus combining tax considerations and mortgage considerations it's likely a better decision to buy a property in your own name if you are in a low tax band & you don't already own a property. If it is your second property, or you have a high income, it may be more profitable to buy your investment property through a LTD.

To make planning easier I've created a smart property tax calculator on my website www.advancetogo.com/taxcalc that helps you compare the options based on your personal circumstances. It lets you put in your annual income to calculate how much tax you'll pay personally and then compares that to if you bought the property through a LTD.

Location, Location, Location

Yay! We've got to the most exciting part, picking your property! Welcome to the hours and hours you're going to spend looking at properties and deciding which one you're going to make your own. This is the most fun chapter in the whole book.

We've talked about deciding to make a property investment, getting a deposit together, and arranging a mortgage, that's a lot of logistics out of the way. This step is where you have the most freedom to choose the property that you love.

There is a lot to cover in this chapter, we're going to split it into two parts, firstly what to look for, and then where you can find it.

This is an investment decision, so it's about making you money. You want to buy a property where every pound you spend will bring you the highest rental back every month. The dream is a low price property with high price rent. The double dream is a low priced property where the value of the property is likely to increase in future. Thankfully if you find the first 'hotspot', you're very likely to find the second. What does that mean?

Let's use the town of Rentopia as an example. Rentopia has some lovely old-fashioned properties that are quite cheap to buy. Recently an eccentric billionaire founded a robotics laboratory in Rentopia. The reason she chose Rentopia hasn't got anything to do with property investment. She chose Rentopia because it's in the countryside, there is a good school for her children, and she likes the local pub.

The new robotics laboratory has created incredible job opportunities and a lot of people are moving to Rentopia. Many of the new residents are in their late 20's and early 30's and have just got new jobs at the research lab. They don't want to buy houses. Some can't afford to, while others are not sure they want to commit to living in Rentopia for the long term. This influx of new people want to rent!

Alas Rentopia is quite small and there are no plans to build more houses in the near future. So, there is limited supply of housing stock and an excess in demand from tenants. In the short term, rent prices are going to rise. Let's imagine that you found a beautiful little stone cottage in Rentopia and that you bought it for a bargain price. Three eager people have just come to look around the property and all want to rent it from you. There isn't much to choose from in Rentopia so these tenants are all very competitive. One of the potential tenants has just secured the job of a lifetime at the research lab, and they are desperate to rent your property. They're relocating from London and the rent you're asking is far less than what they previously paid. After the viewing that tenant calls you and offers to pay 50% more than the asking rental. Wow. You happily accept and they very happily move in.

This is the short term investment dream, you've found a location where property is cheap and due to high demand the rent prices are rising quickly. Giving you the opportunity to make a significant return.

This scenario is also perfect for you in the long term. Three years have gone by, and many of the people who move to Rentopia have decided that they want to stay for the long term, they want to buy!

Remember there haven't been any new homes built in Rentopia so only one thing can happen, buyers have to compete on price and as there is limited supply they push the price of property in Rentopia upwards.

The moral of the story is: if you can find a location with low property prices and high or rising rent prices, it is very likely that in the long term, over 5 to 10 years the house prices in that area will also go up. While this isn't so important if your aspiration is to just buy one property, it is vital if you want to build a little property empire, I explain why rising property prices are important to ambitious investors in my other book, "The Million Pound Portfolio". You should read it… just saying.

So you want an area with low property prices and high rental, these are hard to find. When people recognise them, everyone tries to buy in that area and the property becomes expensive, the rental growth slows and the exciting opportunity shrinks away to nothing.

As a shrewd investor you want to be on the lookout for trends and changes. You want to find these hotspots before everyone else does.

While there are some companies who are using data to predict market changes and to find investment sweet spots, there isn't yet an algorithm that can defeat local knowledge (although that algorithm is probably not far off…). Every year in the UK around 1 million properties are sold, you have a lot of options.

To bring your search into focus, think about locations that you know well. Also think about locations where it is going to be unlikely for a lot of new properties to be built. For example, a city centre is always going to be a safer location to invest than a large area of new-build properties on the outskirts of a city.

So, where are you from? What's going on in your local area? What's changing? Where are the new coffee shops and art galleries opening? Where are the new universities and colleges opening? Where are the new factories and research laboratories opening? Where has the new road, or bridge, or train line just been built, or is just about to be built? Any of these factors can open up a new opportunity, look for them.

You'll know the place when you find it, because it will feel exciting. You will be excited about the opportunity, the potential. Grab that feeling and use it to make things happen. If you're not completely sure that you should trust your gut, then there is a really quick way to check the situation.

Work out the yield of properties in the area you're excited about. Go online and look at how much a property in that area costs to buy, then look at how much a similar property costs to rent. Do the maths. Annual Rental / Property Price * 100 to work out the % yield. If the yield is coming out anywhere around 10% then you've found a hot spot! If the yield is coming out way over 10%, then don't tell a soul, except me...

Now that you know what to look for in an area, it's time to learn where to look! The best place to find an investment property is Rightmove. They have huge coverage, and nearly all the properties that are sold in the UK each year have been advertised with them. I swear by Rightmove, and in particular their property alerts, which send you an email every time a new property that fits your criteria is listed for sale. When creating an alert you can 'draw an area' on the map to pinpoint the exact hotspot location that you want to buy in, and then set a budget that is a little above and below what you're interested in, so you can catch any opportunities that might be around your sweet spot.

Of course there are other online marketplaces, such as Zoopla, On The Market and Gumtree. There are also regional market places, such as www.espc.com (Edinburgh Solicitors Property Centre) a website local to Edinburgh.

If you start networking in property circles you'll also hear about "off market" property opportunities, this is when a property is for sale but is only shared to a small network through word of mouth or private email lists. It's not publicly advertised online. While many investors swear by off-market 'opportunities', I am ALWAYS skeptical. It's so easy for someone selling a property to advertise it for sale on Rightmove, and access an audience of buyers, why would they limit themselves to a small group of potential buyers?

There are reasons for this, people don't want to make it public knowledge that they are selling, or they are in a tough financial situation and want to sell as quickly as possible even at a loss. I'm not comfortable with either of these scenarios, and would recommend staying away from off-market opportunities. If you like the sound of them, the best way to get access is to start networking with your local estate agents.

Another place to look for deals is at property auctions. Auctions are complicated, so we're going to dedicate a whole chapter to understanding them later.

Searching for a property can take a lot of time. It's not like buying a car, where there are millions of brands, models and colours to choose from. It will likely take time for the right property to pop up in your area. If you go on Rightmove and find an incredible investment opportunity in your hot spot on day one, brilliant! Buy it! However I would expect it to take at least 3 months, and more likely 6 months for you to find the right property.

Do not be in a rush. The biggest mistake you can make is buying the wrong property. You want to wait for the right thing to come along and when it does, you need to be prepared to buy it before anyone else. We will talk about the tips and tricks that will let you beat the competition and buy the property in a later chapter...

Viewing Properties

At this point in the property investment process, you'll have spent a lot of time doing desk research. It's time to graduate to a fully licensed field operative, get out into the big bad world. It's a good idea to view a lot of properties, to educate yourself on the market. Look at properties that are a little above and below your budget, also look at properties that are around your hotspot area.

I'm a great believer in serendipity. You might visit a property that is just above your budget, but in chatting to the estate agent you learn that the property was previously sold, but the deal fell through and the vendor (the person selling the property) would actually accept an offer below the asking price. These sorts of things do happen in viewings, and you can land a deal by throwing your net a little wider.

When you're in the supermarket buying fruit, it's very easy to tell the difference between apples and oranges. Comparing properties is much harder, so I've created a spreadsheet of property fundamentals that will help you score properties. You can download it from www.advancetogo.com/which.

You can gather some of the data before seeing the property, for example fundamentals like the price per square meter (PPSM) and the council tax band. Viewing a property in person provides a research opportunity to learn about qualitative characteristics like natural lighting and noise, which are important to record as they have a big impact on value.

A less obvious consideration when viewing properties is predicted maintenance work. Will the old boiler and decrepit windows need replacing or cost a lot to maintain? The value of a property isn't just size and location, condition is important, creating a budget for replacements or repairs will help you compare properties more accurately.

When buying a property everyone knows that location is the most important thing. Not many people know the second most important thing. Person. Who are you buying from? Perhaps you're buying from an investor who has just renovated the property, and will only accept the highest possible offer. Perhaps you're buying from someone who really wants to move urgently and doesn't care about the money, they will accept an offer £20,000 below the asking price just to get rid of the place!

During viewings you must be a detective, not everything you hear is true. I went to look around a property advertised on the market for £440,000. The estate agent told me that the vendor had turned down two offers for significantly over £480,000. I didn't believe it. I offered £448,000 and my offer was accepted by the vendor. £32,000 less than the agent said. Don't believe everything you're told and factor that into your intelligence gathering on viewings.

People will often be funny about sharing information on viewings, perhaps they worry that by saying the wrong thing they might put you off buying. Their worry may be well placed. That is why it's so important that you ask a lot about who is selling and why, so you can uncover any secret information.

Here are some useful information gathering questions: How long have they owned the property? Why did they decide to sell it? Dig into the why with some curious questions;- What does the vendor do now? Where do they live? How does this property fit into their life, and how will the sale of this property affect them? Are they desperate to sell, or will they happily leave the property on the market for 5 years. That is what you want to know but you can't ask exactly that as people will rarely give a straight answer! You can also probe into how long the property has been on the market for.

Don't bother asking the vendor if they have had any offers, if they had a good offer they wouldn't be showing you around, anything they say here is not likely to be useful. For example, I know a vendor who turned down a great offer to sell their property just before the 2008 financial crash. They wanted more money. 6 months later they were wishing they had taken the offer, 12 months later they sold for £80,000 lower than the previous offer, and they were happy to be rid of the property. Imagine if you asked that vendor if they had any offers. They would tell you they had, at such and such price, and that they had turned it down. You'd then be misled about how much they would actually accept for the property. As a super sleuth you have to ask the right questions, and be discriminatory in trusting the answers!

Sometimes you won't be told anything at all, even if you ask, but you can tell who is selling by these clues: if a property has the letter box screwed shut, the gas and water turned off then it most likely means that this property is a repossession (repo). That means the previous owner did not pay their mortgage, and the lender has taken ownership of the property and is selling it. This is great news for you as a buyer because the lender needs to sell the property quickly and is likely amenable to decent offers. I've bought a repo, and I found that making an offer just below the asking price worked well. The lender didn't care about getting the best price possible for the property, they just wanted their money back.

Another way to figure out if the vendor of the property doesn't really care about getting the highest price is to see if it is a sale in probate. This means that the property is being sold by the court. An example would be that an old age pensioner with no family has passed away, and the property is being sold by a representative appointed by the court. This is also good news for you, as the representative has no incentive to get the best possible price, because they won't receive any of the money. They just want to get the property sold and ticked off their to do list, it's a great opportunity to get a good deal. These types of property often end up at auction.

A super quick note about deposits, if you're borrowing money from friends and family and you get on well with them (In this concept I mean they don't boss you around and try to override your decision making processes) then it can be a really good idea to invite them to the viewings so that they can get engaged in the process and excited about you buying your first investment property. Who knows, perhaps after a few viewings they might yet find a few extra thousand pounds to contribute to your deposit! Having someone else with you at the viewing can make it easier to uncover truths, and it can also be useful for spotting maintenance jobs which one person might miss.

When viewing a property I am always looking at how to make it more valuable. A good way to do this is by changing the layout to increase the number of bedrooms. This usually requires renovation work. If you're interested in learning how to renovate properties then read my other book "Making your first £100,000" There are lots more things to think about like load bearing walls, the location of water and waste pipes, and planning regulations.

To summarise, the most important consideration when viewing a property is to ask yourself, would you be happy to live there? You can take a lot of pride in providing good quality rental accommodation. Thinking about a property as a home will help you make profitable decisions in the long term. During viewings, be bold, ask curious questions, don't be bullied out of seeing a property, or be tricked into offering too much money. Take your time with viewings, maybe you will strike lucky and the first property you see will be the one, maybe you have to view 50! When buying such a big asset as property, a small percentage difference in price is a huge amount of money so waiting a few months for a good deal will save tens of thousands of pounds.

Making An Offer

This chapter jumps ahead a step. We're going to learn the process of buying a property, and then come back to negotiating on price. It's important to teach you in this order. To negotiate buying a property, you need to be confident and that comes from understanding the process.

The offer stage is an incredibly exciting part of the journey. So far you've built up your deposit, you've got a mortgage in principle, you've found your hot-spot and the perfect property, what do you do next?

Think about the last time you bought a coffee, you walked into the shop, ordered, tapped your contactless payment, grabbed your coffee and walked out again. It's a very simple transaction, you, the coffee vendor, your money, their coffee... Buying a property is not this easy.

Imagine that you've walked into the coffee shop, and you want to buy a coffee. You can't walk up to the barista and order, instead you have to make an offer through a middleman, the middleman then passes your offer to the barista. The barista accepts, they then have to instruct a lawyer to gather the needed paperwork to prove they own the coffee, the lawyer then creates a contract to sell the coffee. You, the thirsty coffee buyer, now need to get your own lawyer to make sure that the contract to buy this coffee is legit, and that the coffee is actually coffee, and that the barista definitely does own the coffee. This coffee is also incredibly expensive, so you need a bank to lend you money to buy the coffee. The bank also wants to make sure that it's a really good coffee, so they will want to send a trained coffee surveyor in to make sure the deal is good. Then and only then can you sign the contracts, transfer the money, and finally drink the wonderful coffee, which is by now cold.

A property is probably the most expensive thing you will ever buy, and there have been a lot of laws written to protect you, the buyer. When transferring hundreds of thousands, or millions of pounds, you need to be certain that you are actually buying the property, not transferring the money to someone who is a fraudster simply pretending to own it. This is where the lawyers come in.

Lawyers who specialise in property transactions are called conveyancing solicitors. Both sides (the vendor's solicitor and your solicitor) have the same job, to make sure that the vendor owns the property, and that after the money has changed hands, you the buyer will be the legal owner of the property.

It may seem a little crazy that you both need to get lawyers here, but it's a complicated process and a lot can go wrong. In the UK, the government is in charge of making sure that all property transactions are legal. The government maintains a service called The Land Registry. The Land Registry is a centralised authority, that has a list of every single building and plot of land in the whole of the UK, and a list of who owns it. Everything is recorded and stored by the land registry, knowing how old fashioned the property industry is, you might not be surprised to know that the land registry has a lot of paper records.The record that specifies property ownership is called a title deed. This process of transferring ownership of a property is so important that it has an entire subsection of law dedicated to it, welcome to the world of conveyancing.

The job of the vendor's solicitor is to search the land registry, and find the title deed for the property, and check that the person selling it really does own it. Their second job is to verify the exact definition of the property. This is called 'the property envelope'. What does this mean? Imagine that you viewed a house with a huge garden and wanted to buy it, but when the solicitor looked at the title deeds they found out that the garden wasn't actually owned by the vendor, and wouldn't be included in the deal! So the vendor's solicitor has to do a very careful job to check exactly what is being sold. The vendor's solicitor will then create a legally binding contract that confirms the vendor is selling the property to you the buyer, identifies the specific property and the price.

The buyer's solicitor is going to do exactly the same things. They are going to double check the land registry, and review the title deeds to make sure the vendor does own the property, to review exactly what is being sold, and to check if there are any special conditions attached.

A lot can go wrong here. Your solicitor has to search the Local Authority to check planning records. This is done for two reasons, firstly to check that the property you're buying is legal. For example if you're buying a converted factory, did the developers get the planning permission needed to convert the property from commercial use to residential use? The solicitor will also check that the property was built to the relevant building standards, if the property was built recently, or renovated recently, the Local Authority search will show a completion certificate that confirms all works have been inspected by the local council's building control officer and it meets all of the building standards. The Local Authority search should also let you know about any future plans that have been proposed or granted, for instance, are you buying a peaceful property overlooking a huge forest without knowing that planning permission has been granted to build a huge shopping centre opposite? This is an important part of the due diligence process to make sure you know exactly what you're buying! After all of the searches and surveys are done, your solicitor will review the contract to make sure everything is legit and correct. We don't want any funny business or silly errors!

Once everything is in agreement between you (the buyer), the vendor, and both sets of lawyers, you'll sign the contract, and transfer over the money to the vendor. Once they have the money, you get the keys. Your lawyer will then update the title deeds and will let the land registry know that you're the new owner! That is the deal done. So the simple version of a property transaction has four parties, a vendor, the vendor's solicitor, a buyer, the buyer's solicitor.

Most transactions are a little more complicated, they usually have eight parties: a vendor, the vendor's estate agent, the vendor's solicitor, a buyer, the buyer's solicitor, the mortgage broker, the lender, and the lender's surveyor. Now you're starting to have a good idea about why property transactions can be complicated and slow!

Let's go through the more complicated version of a transaction, so you know exactly what is going on and the order in which you'll likely meet everyone.

Let's assume that you're buying the property using a mortgage, it's time to meet the broker, and the lender. The lender will take you through a process to see if they think you are 'creditworthy' aka 'will you actually be able to pay them back'. They will then decide how much money they are comfortable lending you. They'll then create a 'Mortgage in Principle', and give you a mortgage certificate. This is a document that confirms they are happy to lend to you, and will state how much money they will lend, for how long and the mortgage rate.

You'll start searching the market for a property and you'll book some viewings, that's when you'll meet the estate agent, lucky you! The estate agent will normally ask you for more details about your circumstances. Their questions will include;- are you a cash buyer, do you need a mortgage, and do you have to sell your current house. The answers to these questions change the quality of your offer. The best position is to be a cash buyer, as you're not reliant on getting mortgage approval, or waiting for your house to sell. If you need a mortgage, the estate agent will ask if you have a 'Mortgage in Principle'. If your offer is subject to you selling your current property, this is called being in a chain, and it's the worst position to be in.

When you find a property you love, you'll let the estate agent know that you want to make an offer. This needs to be done in writing so that it's recorded and so the agent can send it to the vendor. When your offer is accepted, the estate agent will then want to know which solicitor you are using, we'll go into how you choose the right solicitor in more detail in a minute. At this stage you're not committed to buying the property and you can still pull out of the deal. You pulling out is a risk to the estate agent and they will want to see commitment in the form of you paying the solicitor to start the conveyancing process.

We're now going to bring another player into the game. The surveyor. When you're buying using a mortgage, the lender will want to send out an independent third party to verify the property value. Sometimes the lender will pay for the valuation, sometimes you'll have to cover the cost which can range from £200 to £800.

Let's pause to better understand the role of the surveyor. Perhaps you see a property on the market for £500,000 and you want to buy it, the vendor agrees to sell it to you for that price, and the lender agrees to give you 90% of the money £450,000. Well the lender wants to make sure that the property is worth £500,000. What would happen if you and the vendor both thought the property was worth £500,000 but, after buying it, you lost your job, and you couldn't make the mortgage payments? Then the lender has to repossess and sell the property to get their money back. Disaster, shock and horror. No one else thinks that the property is worth £500,000, there is a huge problem with the roof which will cost £100,000 to fix. If the lender has to sell the property which is now worth £400,000 the lender stands to lose £50,000 as do you! So the lender wants to make sure that the price agreed for the property is fair, and safe for them, they don't want to risk losing the money they are lending you to buy the property. The lender will only give you the money if the surveyor agrees with the price.

The next thing the estate agent wants to know, do you really have the deposit money?! They will want to see a bank statement, or a screenshot of a bank account that shows you have the deposit cash needed to buy the property. Last but not least, the estate agent has to make sure you are not a money launderer and will need to run an Anti Money Laundering (AML) check to prove your ID and source of funds.

To recap, you've made an offer to the estate agent, the vendor has accepted, you've instructed a solicitor, paid the lender to do the survey, and sent the estate agent proof that you have the money and you've passed the AML check.

It's now time for your solicitor to do some work, they will get busy with searches in a number of online databases checking for risks like: is the property in a flood zone, have renovation works have been done to standard, are there unpaid repair bills, is the property built on an old landfill site, is there a public right of way path through your back garden? If you're buying an older building, your solicitor may recommend that you get a structural survey conducted by an engineer, or a damp survey, or a wood survey, or roof survey, or all of them.

The vendor's solicitor is responsible for putting together the contract. In Scotland this part of the contract is called 'the missives', in other places it's called a Deed of Sale, or simply a contract. Your solicitor is then responsible for reviewing the contract and making sure there isn't anything weird in it. It is important to be really clear on the contract, it can also include provisions for the sale of fixtures and fittings. For instance are the lovely Smeg fridge and Whirlpool dishwasher included in the sale, or will the vendor take them out?

Your offer is not legally binding until the contracts are signed, that means, at any stage until you sign, you can pull out of the deal.

In the contract a date will be set called the completion date. Normally this is 6-8 weeks in the future, it gives the mortgage company time to process everything and gives you the time to plan the move in. On the completion date, you have to transfer all of the money to the vendor. In practise what happens is that you transfer the deposit money to your solicitor, who holds it in their client account, the lender then also pays money to the solicitor's client account, and your solicitor then transfers all of the money, minus their fee, to the vendor's solicitor. On the completion date, you're given the keys!

When the money has all changed hands, your solicitor will put your name on the title deed. Depending on the situation, the solicitor can store the title deed for you, they will also register it electronically with the land registry. If you're borrowing money, the lender will often hold the title deed on your behalf. The lender will also have something called, the first charge over the property. That means that the lender will get paid before anyone else, when the property is sold in the future. This is important because in the rare situation where a property falls in value, if you sell for less than you bought, you will take the loss, not the lender!

When you move in there is usually a 5-10 day window during which you can report any maintenance problems and the vendor has to pay for them. Once again, check the fine print as these details will be in the contract and they are important. What happens if you move in and then 4 days later the boiler breaks and costs £4,000 to fix? You don't want to have to pay for that!

You've got a good idea of the process, and probably understand it better than a lot of people who work in the property industry! Something I promised we would come back to earlier, how should you select a solicitor? This is a really tricky question. There are really two considerations, how diligent the solicitor will be at doing the searches and finding any problems for you and how much they will charge? A good conveyancing solicitor will cost around £1,000 if you're paying a lot more than that, you are paying too much. It's a fair idea to ask the estate agent for a recommendation of a good solicitor, but many estate agents get a referral commission from the conveyancer, so they are likely to be biased.

How can you tell if a solicitor is diligent and will do the best job possible for you? I've got a neat little rule of thumb to use here. People who enjoy their job usually do their jobs better than people who don't. So get chatty with each solicitor you call, ask them how long they have been doing the job, ask them if they have any good tips or suggestions for you, ask them what they think of the property market at the moment, if they have any nightmare stories of things going wrong. Also, note how easy or difficult it actually was to get through to speak with them. Then pick the one you enjoyed speaking with the most, they will likely do you the best job. If you get a grumpy solicitor with no stories and no advice, who has no passion or will to live, they probably don't really care about you buying your first investment property and you shouldn't work with them.

Negotiating With Fear & Greed

Negotiation tactics need to be used with caution. The risk is you get greedy and try to over optimise at the expense of your goals. If a property is on the market at a fixed price of £200,000 and you think it is worth £200,000, don't mess around. Get the deal done and start executing your property investment strategy, don't try and buy it for £199,000 and waste time haggling.

So how do you know what a property is worth? First start by setting your target yield. I always want to get a gross rental yield of 10% or more. If I know that a property will rent for £20,000 a year, then I think that the fair price of that property is £200,000. I think of property value using a traffic light system. If the rental yield is much higher than the interest rate I am paying the bank, then it's a 'Green Light Deal'. For example, if interest rates are at 3% and I can buy a property at a price that creates a 10% yield, then I am benefiting from a powerful compound interest differential of 7%. Any property value that makes the yield marginally above the bank's interest rate is amber. For instance, if I pay £500,000 for a property that makes £20,000 in rental then I have a 4% yield, if the bank's interest rate is 3% I am still benefiting from compound interest, however it is risky. If interest rates go up by more than 1%, I will start to lose money. Red light deals are any price that causes the rental yield to be lower than the bank's interest rate.

Changing your target yield will have a big impact on the value you attribute to a property. If you know the property will rent for £20,000 and you want a yield of 10% then you will pay £200,000 to buy it. If you want a yield of 9% then the property becomes worth £222,222. It is important to be firm with your target yields, drop them too low and you'll over-value the property and put yourself at risk of losing money.

By the time you're ready to offer on a property you may be overly enthusiastic. You've got money burning a hole in your pocket and you urgently want to buy. This excitement is dangerous, it can make you become desperate to buy causing you to over-pay. The price you've worked out at your lowest acceptable yield must be your maximum price. Any price above that is not acceptable. Be firm here. If your maximum price is £250,000 and you get told that you can buy it for £255,000 you must say no. This is really hard, but the reason why you are doing all of this work is to make a profit, and paying too much means you won't.

The majority of properties sold on the market are in the red light investment zone, they don't make financial sense and are not good deals. Often you will see properties in the amber zone but it's hard to find properties in the green zone. Great investment deals don't appear often. To be successful as a property investor you have to make them happen by negotiating.

When properties are advertised they often come with different promotions for example: Fixed Price, Offers Over, Guide Price, Offers In The Region Of, Offers In Excess Of. You can ignore all of these labels. Each of them means the exact same thing, 'For Sale'. If a property says offers over £200,000 and you offer £190,000 the estate agent is legally bound to share the offer with the vendor. In-fact no matter what you offer the agent must pass it to the vendor for them to consider. The vendor can accept any offer at any time even if it's not the highest offer. As you are a property investor getting the best possible price is your number one objective. So let's dig into negotiation tactics and your offer strategy.

Knowledge is power, to negotiate successfully you need information and you need to be communicating with the right people. Your objective is to negotiate directly with the vendor as they are the ultimate decision maker. Agents and solicitors will often try to block you from accessing the decision maker. Don't let their attempts at authority cloud the situation, you are the buyer, so you have all the power. One of the reasons why the middle men try and block contact is that they don't want the vendor to reveal any sensitive information that might affect the negotiations.

Imagine that you are a CIA operative, your first objective in the negotiations is to gather information. You need to pump everyone for as much intel as possible. The best source is the vendor themselves, but useful information can often be picked up from the estate agent or the vendor's solicitor.

There is an important caveat to remember, you want to tell the other side as little information about you as possible. If you make a low offer on a property, but during the viewing you let slip that "you've been searching the market for 8 months and this is the only property that you've seen that you like, and that you are absolutely in love with it..." then the vendor will hold out for you to make a better offer because they know how much you want the property. You've put the power in their hands by giving them too much information!

You're not a lone agent in your intelligence gathering mission. Get an 'impartial' third party, like your solicitor, to speak to the estate agent and ask what the vendor would actually sell for, or what's really going on with the sale? The selling estate agent is your adversary, they want to sell at a high price, you want to buy at a low one.

Gathering this information will help you decide which negotiating tactic or tactics to use when making an offer. Not all tactics will work with all types of vendors. The more you know about the vendor and the situation, the better you'll be able to move the negotiations to your advantage.

Some of the example questions you can ask: Why are they selling? Is it their family home that they loved? Have they bought a new house already? Do they need to sell this to buy? Do they have a timeline that they have to move by?

We gather this information because it helps us to control the mechanics that make deals happen. Two emotions control financial negotiations: fear and greed. As a buyer and a newly minted negotiation aficionado you don't want to let emotions affect you. You're not afraid of losing out on a deal, and you're not so greedy that you'll miss out on a deal by offering too low either. You have to temper your emotions with logic. If at any point you're struggling to do this, use maths. Sit down and calculate the yield of the property and decide if you like the numbers. Taking the time to do that will calm your emotional mind so you can focus on the numbers rather than your feelings.

When you view a property, watch out for the other side trying to manipulate your emotions. Estate agents, and vendors will tell you "Oh there has been a lot of interest" this is to make you fear that someone else will buy it before you. Another manipulation you'll hear a lot, "This is the only property in the area that has a..." again trying to make a property seem rare is a way of increasing your fear of missing out on something special. When you're aware that the other side will likely try to manipulate your emotions you can guard against it, and ensure you are not pushed into a bad deal.

Conversely to get a good deal you want the vendor to feel more fear than greed. During a viewing you might find yourself saying, "the property around the corner is cheaper and has more space" making the vendor fear that no one will buy their property at the price it's being advertised. If the vendor is greedy they will hold out for a high price and will turn down reasonable offers because they want more money.

The vendor's biggest fear is not being able to sell their property at all. What if lots of properties come on the market and theirs doesn't sell? What if no one likes their property? What if there is a recession and house prices crash? If the vendor thinks house prices are going to go down, they will fear financial loss and will be motivated to sell at a lower price before the bubble bursts.

Although it might sound harsh, fear is the subconscious emotion that you want the vendor to have. Most negotiation tactics play around triggering this emotion in the vendor. Let's look through some common examples when a vendor may have mounting fears.

The best example is when an agreed sale falls through. The vendor has been on an emotional rollercoaster: excited about the sale, anxious when it starts to go wrong, disappointed at the fall through, exhausted at the prospect of going back on the market and extremely fearful that the next deal might also fall through. If you see that a property has come back on the market it's a great time to make an offer below asking. The agent and vendor both urgently want to get the deal done and their fear state is high, they will likely accept offers that previously would have been rejected.

One of the least known statistics in the property world is that almost half of all property deals fall through. Every time that I offer on a property and I don't win it, I stay in touch with the estate agent to let them know I am still interested in buying in case the deal does fall through. I bought my very first property using this process. It was on the market for £95,000 I offered £87,000, another buyer offered £105,000. I lost. Two months later the estate agent called me and asked if my original offer was still on the table. I accepted and benefited from a below market value green light deal. Following up with the agent keeps you at the top of their list of people to call in the event of a fall through and gives you a huge financial advantage as an investor.

Deals that fall through often create time related urgency especially if the vendor is in a chain. A property chain is when one transaction relies on another. For example, Mrs. Potter is selling her house because she has a baby on the way and needs to buy a bigger house. Mrs. Potter has found the perfect new house and had her offer accepted, but she won't have enough money to buy the perfect new house until she's sold her current one. She has to sell in four months or the perfect new house will be put back on the market. The situation creates the fear of losing the perfect new house. As time runs out, Mrs. Potter will be open to lower offers as the need to sell becomes more urgent, she will also prioritise offers that are less likely to fall through, even if they are not the best financial offer available.

If the vendor doesn't have a timeline, you can create your own time pressure on a deal. This is difficult to do in a strong market where the vendor has lots of offers coming in, but it can be very effective in a slow market. Put an offer in and let the vendor know that you've also offered on another property and you'll continue with the first to accept. This creates urgency and fear, by not accepting your offer, the vendor risks having their property on the market for a long time without selling.

Now that you've got a good understanding of the emotions and situations that drive deals, let's start to look at more practical negotiation tactics you can implement.

One of the most powerful is 'likeability'. People have an unconscious bias to do deals with people they like, and people who are similar to them. It can be hard to leverage this in your negotiations if you're not similar to the vendor and have no reason to like one another. To utilise this tactic make sure you are not being unlikeable. Don't be an ass. Treat the vendor with respect, if you're making a low offer on the property justify why so they don't think you're trying to take advantage of them.

This brings us onto justification. "I am making you a lower offer" doesn't sound good. "I am making you a lower offer because…" is much stronger and will succeed more often. If you want to offer below the asking price, you can justify your offer by showing the vendor comparable properties that are on the market right now or that have recently sold. This can bring a vendor back down to earth if they have priced their property too high. It also heightens their fear that no one will buy their property if there are cheaper or better options on the market. You can use this tool on my website www.advancetogo.com/comparables to see comparable properties that are on the market and to find the house price changes over time in an area.

Another good justification can be explaining the work that you'll need to do in order to move into the property. Ask for access and get a builder to quote for the work you're thinking of. For example, "We really love the house but it doesn't have enough space for us. If we put a conservatory on, it would be perfect but that would cost £X thousand, here is a quote from a builder." This shows you're seriously interested in the house and helps the vendor justify in their own mind why they should sell the house to you for less than they have advertised it. When used in the right scenario it can be highly compelling.

Next up is the 'Cash' offer. Buying in cash is a very powerful negotiation tool. We've established that vendors have a fear that the deal will fall through. This can be caused by many reasons, but the most common are: the person buying needs a mortgage and that bank rejects them; and the person buying is in a chain and their house doesn't sell in time. The safest option for the vendor is to choose the 'cash' offer. This is when the buyer has all of the money needed accessible to pay right away, thus reducing the chance of a fall through.

If you're not buying in cash, and you need to buy with a mortgage, you can still use this as a negotiating advantage by having a 'Mortgage in Principle'. You can then send this mortgage certificate to the estate agent to show that you're a credible buyer and that you're able to make the deal happen.

It's hard to negotiate in a 'hot' market when lots of people are offering above you. Even then you still can win deals by using these tactics. Leverage the fact you are a low risk cash buyer, or have a mortgage in principle arranged, use time and the vendor's circumstances to your advantage. Follow up even if you lose out to catch deals that fall through before they get back on the market, and don't be an ass.

Buying at Auction

Here is a phrase I love "The odds are good, but the goods are odd." It perfectly describes finding a green light deal at a property auction. As a rule of thumb if a property was normal it wouldn't be in an auction, nearly all properties sold at auction have some kind of history, they are the odd ones. That strangeness provides an opportunity to find deals!

A property auction is a true cultural melting pot, the lure of a bargain drags in everyone from bricklayers to barons. It's not uncommon to find a workman in painty overalls sitting next to a well dressed lady showing off expensive jewellery. People from all walks of life are all competing at the same thing, property investment.

Most auctions are normally held in low cost venues, these can be football clubs, golf clubs, or airport hotels, everything about auctions is budget, from the venue to the instant coffee. This is the grubby part of the property market, miles away from fancy high street estate agents who will offer you barista coffee when you walk through the door.

With auctions you have to do your research in advance. When buying a normal property, you can make an offer and then pull out from the deal later if your solicitor finds something strange during the due-diligence. This isn't the case with property auctions. When you bid, you're committed to buying the property. If you pull out, you'll have to pay a hefty fee, usually 10% of the property price. This means you have to do all the due diligence before you make a bid.

I've bought properties without looking around them in person. If I know the area well, I like the floor plan, the home report and am happy with the property photographs then I am comfortable making an offer without going to see the property in person. This isn't the case with auction properties. It's vital that you go and see the property in person. There is some unknown reason why the property isn't on the open market, so it's important to go to an open day, or a viewing to make sure the property is as you expect. You can't pull out later.

The real homework is reading the property's legal pack. Usually when a property is sold, all of the legal review happens after the price is agreed and this can take months. In an auction the vendor has to have all of their legal documentation prepared before they can sell. This means each property will have a legal pack that contains every single piece of information that is required to complete the conveyancing process, meaning the transaction can happen much faster, usually within two weeks.

Hiding somewhere in this long and purposefully boring documentation will be the reason why this property is being sold at auction. Let's go through a quick handful of reasons why properties might be at auction so you've got an idea of what to look out for. The property may have been renovated by a developer that did not get planning permission, or hasn't attained a building warrant. This would mean a lot of money and time needs to be spent to make the building compliant and legal for someone to rent. It might be that the property has a very small floor area, has some kind of structural damage, or isn't currently habitable. This means that most banks won't lend you money to buy the property. If it's not possible to get a mortgage on a property then you can only buy it in cash. It could be that the owner has died and has no relatives, this is called a sale in probate. Perhaps the previous owner didn't make their mortgage payments and the property was repossessed by the lender. There will be a reason, sometimes two reasons! So make sure you find and understand them, before you consider making a bid.

Many companies specialise in pre-auction pack analysis. So if you find a property you like, you attend a viewing and it looks amazing, then you might want to pay for a solicitor to review the property's legal pack before the auction so you can be sure you've discovered why it is being sold at auction.

The first time you buy a property at auction can be very dangerous. It's incredibly important to remember the impact of tax and fees. For example if you have a strict £350,000 budget, then it is important for you to know you can't bid £350,000 in the auction! This is because you have to add on the auction's fees and the tax costs to the final property price. For example bidding £350,000 for the property will likely attract these extra costs: 1% auction fee £3,500 and land tax £7,500. This means your total property cost will be £360,000. A whopping £10,000 over the hammer price.

As with all auction situations, make sure that you've decided what your best and final offer will be before you get sucked into the competitive atmosphere of the auction house. Write this down on a piece of paper, and work out the tax and auction fee on top of your best offer. Then stay firm and don't bid more than that.

Before the auction starts you'll have to listen to the terms and conditions. In general when you win a property you have to pay a 10% deposit immediately. Not that evening, not tomorrow, but right then and there. That means if you just offered £350,000 for a property you have to be able to pay £35,000 by bank transfer or credit card. Kinda scary right…! What is even more terrifying is if you don't come up with the rest of the cash usually in 7 to 14 days, then you lose your 10% deposit! This is why it is so important to be prepared when buying at auction. If you need a mortgage to buy the property, you have to make sure that the mortgage funds will be ready in the required time period. One day late and the auction company will take your deposit and smile at you while they do it. People in property don't mess around and if you're not properly prepared it can be a financial catastrophe.

The mechanics of bidding at auction are very straight forward. You can turn up to the auction, walk into the room without saying a word to anyone and then start bidding by raising your hand and getting the auctioneer's attention. There is usually no registration process at the start. Although this may vary depending on the auction company. Once you've won the bid, then an assistant from the auction company will descend on you like a vulture upon carrion, with a clip board and registration form. They will whizz you off to a quieter part of the building to fill out the paperwork and make the 10% deposit payment. It really is as fast as that!

So now you understand how the auction works and that there are risks. The goods are odd and you must make an irreversible financial commitment, 10% of the purchase price, that you will lose if you pull out later in the process or if you don't pay the full balance in time!

Aside from the chance to get a bargain, the other draw to auctions is the competitive aspect! If you want to buy at auction I recommend attending at least one auction in advance so you understand just how powerful this competitive environment is.

Like every pearl of wisdom I depart to you in this book dear reader, we are always looking for the unfair advantages that can get you the best financial return on your property investment. Yes, there are tactics you can employ when bidding to improve your chances of winning a property at the best price.

While you might be thinking of trying to divert traffic from the auction venue so that you're the only attendee there to bid, that may cross over ethical and legal lines. So instead we will look at mental tools you can use to bully your opponents into submission.

Let's think about animals in the wild. Why do birds plume out their feathers, why do cats arch their backs, why do puffer fish puff? Animals know that the best way to win a fight is to intimidate your opponent by making yourself appear bigger and more dangerous than they are. In auctions you need to get primal and scare off your competitors.

Make sure you are well dressed and visible, it's beneficial to attend the auction with a number of friends and family. You look much more powerful in a group of five than you do on your own. You want the other bidders to see you and to fear competing against you.

Always make the first bid. Making the first bid will show everyone in the room that you are in charge and will make sure everyone knows that you want the property. This gives you a psychological advantage as the next bidder has to come in as your competitor. Many people advise waiting for others to make the first bid and then jumping in at the end. I advise that you make the first bid, then wait until the end. It's like planting a flag in the sand. You're letting everyone know you want the property but you then let other bidders fight amongst each other and only come back in at the end.

When bidding first, the auctioneer will try to suck you into a bidding war. They will try to do this by using time pressure and creating a lot of pace and momentum. Don't play their game, enjoy the awkward silence. You can always jump in at the last minute and the auctioneer will give you this chance by advising they are about to sell. They will give you the "going, going, gone".

It's really hard to resist the power of the auctioneer, they are a professional trained in getting people to frantically bid up the prices. There are two things you can do here that put you in control of the auction.

The auctioneer will normally increase the price in jumps of a round number. So when a property is for sale at £165,000 after the first bid the auctioneer will ask for an offer of £5,000 above. They will say "Can I get £170,000?". Normally they will continue in jumps of £5,000, but if there is a bit of competition in the room they will jump up to £10,000. So when someone says "yes I bid £170,000", they then "asks can I get £180,000". The way you can control the situation is by making an offer to the auctioneer either below or above what they have asked for.

Let's imagine that property is on at £165,000 and you come in with the first bid. The auctioneer then asks for £170,000 and your competition jumps in. Now the auctioneer thinks you're keen because you bid first, he's going to try and push you into a higher number so he is going to ask for £180,000 creating momentum. You can verbally counter offer, you don't have to just wave your hand to bid, you can speak.

You can control the auction and slow down the pace by shouting out £175,000. The auctioneer will hate you for doing this as they are trying hard to create competition. You counter offering puts you in power, it shows your competitors that you are controlling the situation and it stops the auctioneer creating a competitive pace.

The other option you have is to jump bid. This is a real power move. Sticking to the same scenario. The auctioneer is asking you for £180,000. Perhaps you've decided that the top price you would pay for this property is £233,000. You want to get it as cheaply as possible but you know it's going to be competitive. You think that £215,000 is a really good price. The auction started at £165,000. The auctioneer now has a bid of £170,000 against you and is asking you for £180,000. A jump bid is when you shout out a much higher offer than the auctioneer is asking for. For example when they ask for £180,000 you shout out £215,000. This is a massive jump of £45,000. It is going to confuse and scare off your competition. Jump bids are risky, perhaps your competition would have stopped bidding at £200,000, or perhaps they would have stopped at £240,000. The jump bid shows your competition that you want the property no matter what and that you're not just trying to get the best deal. It should make them lose hope of winning and scare them off, as they believe that you will just keep bidding. You must be crazy if you offered so much more than the next bid, so they should give up now.

Like all tactics in this book, they depend on the scenario and your comfort level. You could start an auction by bidding first, then staying out the way until the property is almost sold, then jumping in with an offer slightly lower than the auctioneer wanted. If your competitor then starts to bid against you, you could use a jump bid to scare them off.

Just as I told you to write down your best and final offer on a piece of paper, most other people will also have a top price they are willing to pay. These top prices are often a round number, this creates a strategic risk. For example if the property is starting at £165,000 and you and your opponent both have a top price of £200,000 you want to make sure that you're not the person who offers £190,000 because then the auctioneer will ask for £200,000 which your opponent will give, and when the auctioneer asks you for £210,000 it will be above your best and final price and you will lose. Make sure that either you bid the round number, or your top price is just over. This is a perfect example of when to use a jump bid. If your opponent is on £180,000 and the auctioneer asks for £190,000 and your top budget is £200,000 you should jump bid and offer £200,000. Alternatively set your budget at £205,000 and then when your competition bids their maximum of £200,000 and the auctioneer asks you for £210,000 you can come back and offer the auctioneer £205,000 which they will accept!

Auctions are dangerous but also very fun, spend some time attending them before you actually want to buy and make sure you know exactly what tactics you will use because in the heat of battle your bidding war will pass in a blink.

Maximising Rental & Minimising Management

You've put a lot of energy into your property and it's about to pay off. With one final task your investment will start making money, it's time to find your tenants.

This is a fun part of the property investment process, you turn a property into a desirable home. Most landlords don't put much love into their properties. The bad landlords rent out dirty, poorly maintained ones. While the good landlords rent out clean but boring properties that are furnished top to bottom with Ikea furniture. The great landlords, like you, create homes where people want to live. They put in a little more thought and a little more love. As a result… they earn a lot more rent!

When preparing a property to rent out you want to choose a design aesthetic that will appeal to a large audience. At the same time you need to keep costs low and remember maintenance.

For all these reasons I urge you to paint walls white! You're going to be renting this property for years, and during that time you're going to need to repaint walls. If you get some special colour, that is then out of stock, or discontinued it will be really annoying as you can't do any touch up work, instead you'll have to repaint whole rooms a new colour. Also no one hates white walls, and they make flats look bright and spacious.

Look for clean, sturdy and matching furniture that fits a consistent design style throughout the property. I love shopping for things on Gumtree as second hand furniture usually saves you a lot of money. My choice is normally for antique wooden furniture that has already been 'well loved', because it's already marked and worn, it won't look out of place in a few years. I know other investors who prefer all modern furniture and love a more contemporary look, it's up to you! Whatever you settle on, make it look well thought-out and organised, not just randomly thrown together. Do give a flat some cute homely touches, perhaps put a few books on the book shelves, maybe buy a couple of low maintenance plants. However don't over clutter places.

When you've got your property looking perfect (remember perfection is knowing when to stop) then you're going to need to take photos for advertising. There are a couple of things I like to do when taking photos to really make things pop. Wait for a sunny day, lighting is the key to making rooms look good. Even if it is the sunniest day of the year, turn every light in the place on. If you're sceptical about this try taking photos with the lights off and on again with them on, and see which look better. #toldyouso.

I also love to take some bright colourful flowers with me, and show them off in the communal spaces. I often take one bunch of flowers and move them from room to room when taking the photos.

It's also a chance for you to do some lovely brand association, this is a small point but it makes a difference. Think aspirational lifestyle. If you're taking some photos of the kitchen, bring a nice bottle of champagne with you and make sure it's visible in the photos. It almost goes without saying but, make sure the place is spotlessly clean and make sure that beds are made up, curtains drawn back and that the property looks fabulous.

I use an ultra-wide angle lens (12mm) on a Canon DSLR to take property photos, however most mobile phone cameras are so good that you'll likely be able to use one. If you really want to go crazy, you can hire a property photographer, it depends on your budget. I'd encourage you to try taking the photos yourself and see how you get on. Once you've got some photos, do take the time to play with editing them. Even if it's as simple as putting them through an Instagram filter to increase the brightness or contrast. Remember you are in sales mode and you have to make your property look good, it's worth putting in these extra touches of effort as it's going to make you more money in rental.

If you want to stand out from the crowd I'd recommend getting a virtual tour created. These are not as crazy expensive as you might think. I recommend the £95, 360 tour offered by a nationwide company called Viewber. This creates a virtual walk through of the property and shows the whole property in a three dimensional 'dolls house'. Check my website www.advancetogo.com/tour for an example.

There is one very important reason why you should put a lot of time and energy into these property photos. Your property will never look as good again! As soon as tenants move in there will be wear and tear. You want to take photos now and use them for the next five plus years. You don't want to have to take advertising photos every year!

It's also really useful to have a floor plan of the property, this helps people get a good idea of the size and the layout. It saves you from having time wasters come view, if they don't like the layout and can learn that from just looking at the floor plan online.

Once you've got the photos you now need to write a description. This is another opportunity to add in some character, and stand out from the crowd. This isn't hard. Most descriptions are written by tired estate agents. They will contain phrases like 'delighted to offer this well presented property', or 'kitchen benefits from ample storage' or 'comprises three rooms'. These descriptions are so dull. If you add a little sparkle, you'll catch more eyes. "This is a quirky home with a marble bathroom and underfloor heating" or "Our kids love the heated floor, and yours will too". Remember it's about selling a lifestyle, you want to be aspirational.

A quick and very important note, there is a lot of legislation surrounding letting properties and depending on your area there may be legal requirements that you have to meet before you can advertise your property to let. For example in the UK you must have a valid EPC, (Energy Performance Certificate). Other considerations are, electrical and fire safety certification and gas safety certificates. I highly recommend checking with your local council to see if you need to register as a landlord with them, and to find out what local legislation you may have to comply with!

So, you've got the stunning photos, you've done the legal compliance... where should you advertise?

There is only one place, OpenRent. www.openrent.co.uk is a low cost online letting agent. They post your advert on Rightmove, Zoopla and Gumtree. Ensuring that you get the best coverage possible and attract the best selection of tenants.

There isn't a one size fits all way of managing tenant enquiries. It really depends on the type of property that you are renting out. Perhaps you've decided to rent out a family property, with a garden, a play room and a garage. Or perhaps you're renting out a super high end penthouse with a bar and world class sound system. Different types of tenants will have different expectations, some will expect to be able to call and speak to you right away and then view the property the same day.

This isn't my way. When we discussed earlier what type of property to buy, we agreed the best place was a hot spot, with an excess of demand. This means lots of tenants who all want to rent in the same area. Good examples of this are university towns, or cities with a large population of young working professionals. Students and young working professionals are my favourite types of tenants.

We'll run through some tactics to help you earn the highest rental. If these tips don't fit your personal style, ethics, or the type of property you're trying to rent you don't have to use them.

I don't take any phone calls. I make everyone email me. Why? I don't want to have the same conversation 10 or 15 times. At this stage I don't want to hear a tenant's life story. They haven't even seen the property yet, so there isn't any point in starting to build rapport or foster a relationship.

Stage one is really simple, tenants will want to see around your beautiful property. You need to start the landlord tenant relationship off on your terms. I am really, really serious about this. You don't want to take abuse from your tenants, and you really don't want demanding tenants that are going to call you 24/7. Of course just like any service business, in property the customer is always right. Luckily you get to choose the customer so make sure you filter to find the good! There is a process for filtering these out.

Don't let the tenant dictate the viewing availability. Choose a date and time that suits you to do the viewing and then tell the tenant when they can come to look around. I always make these viewing slots about two to three weeks after I first list the property. There is an important reason for this that I will get to in a bit.

If the tenant can not come at that date and time, tell them you are really sorry, but for now that is the only viewing.

It's time to let out a little evil laugh, "muahahah". Not only can the tenants not reach you on the phone, but you are also only giving them one time to view the property. This might sound harsh, but it is a good thing. Don't worry about scaring tenants away, humans in general are attracted to confidence and to scarcity. Your viewing strategy successfully portrays both.

If the tenant can't come to the viewing slot you've selected, apologise and tell them that if the property does not let at that viewing, you will schedule another one with them, but explain that this is really unlikely as a lot of other tenants have enquired.

You may be surprised by the number of tenants who all of a sudden are able to take time off work, change their schedule or send someone around to look for them. This sorts out the serious from the speculative.

Ahead of the viewing you need to email detailed instructions to every potential tenant. In life, I believe, if it can go wrong, it will go wrong. To combat 'Sod's law', take the time to provide the full address and write detailed instructions on how to find it. E.g. "The main door is blue and it's between the Tesco and the Pub". Make it easy for people to find the property. It's easy for people to get lost especially when they are nervous and rushing. You won't want to be on the phone giving directions while trying to show around another group of tenants

In the viewing confirmation email and the viewing reminder email, tell people that they will not be able to call you during the viewing. Let them know if they have any questions about the property or about finding the property, to please email you in advance.

It's also good to think through the common questions and pre-empt them. When is the move in date? How long is the lease? How much is the electricity and gas? How much is the council tax? It's good practise to include all of this information on the advert and to reiterate it in the viewing emails. I also find it useful to be completely transparent about any potential issues with the property. E.G. it's above a pub and can be noisy in the evenings. Let people know well in advance.

In the viewing confirmation email, I include a link to an online application form. We'll touch on the application form in a few paragraphs. It's important.

There are some very powerful reasons why you've made people wait to view, and scheduled the viewing so everyone has to come around in a group. Let's do a mini master class on human psychology. Humans use social proof to make decisions. If you're out for dinner and you walk past an empty restaurant, it's probably not a great place to eat, however, that full restaurant with people queuing outside must be a good place, right? This is social proof, if lots of other people are doing something, it validates that it's good.

We're using that exact same 'busy restaurant' tactic in letting your property. If there are a lot of people all viewing the property it must be good. Having lots of people attend the viewing also gives you other psychological benefits. People value things highly when they are scarce. E.G. diamonds are expensive because they are rare. If they were as common as pebbles on a beach, they wouldn't be valuable. Your property is a scarce commodity. You've made it unique and there is only one available to let, only one group of tenants can rent it!

These two psychological laws fuel a third, rivalry. This is key to getting the best rental price for your property. You've engineered a brilliant situation, lots of people will all come around one flat, showing it's popular and they all know only one group can get it, so they will become competitive and will all want to rent it.

I recommend that you create this situation and then use it to your advantage. Let tenants compete on the rental price. This is pure capitalism, free market forces at their best. If one group of tenants is willing and able to pay more rent for the property, then let them! This is the only way to find out the true rental value of your property, let people compete.

To create this situation I will often advertise my properties at a little below their market rental. For instance if a property let for £2,100 per month the year before, I will advertise it at £1,900 per month so I can get the most people round. Perhaps you feel uncomfortable with this strategy. It is indeed using human psychological hacks to get the best price for your property. I don't believe it to be unethical in the slightest. Tenants have a lot of rental choices and if they don't want to rent from you, or they think the price is too high, then they can go elsewhere. Making a profit from property investment is hard, and you have to put in a lot of work, I urge you to use every tactic possible to make sure that you can profit from your investment.

Conducting a large group viewing can be a little stressful. Perhaps you are showing around 15 or 20 people. It's a lot. Depending on the size of the property, I will often ask for half the group to wait outside, while I show the first half around.

I like to keep the viewing process simple, I shake every tenant's hand while looking them in the eyes and introducing myself. I then tell them to have a look around the property on their own and to come ask me if they have any questions.

If you want to have zero interaction with tenants, or you live geographically far from your investment property, that is completely okay, you can use a brilliant service called Viewber, where a professional viewing agent will show tenants around and gather their feedback for you.

In my near 20 years of property experience I've found that potential tenants do not want you to walk around the property with them, breathing down their necks. They want to look around in their own time, talk about the good and bad parts of the property and be able to do this in a relaxed atmosphere.

Potential tenants will come and ask questions, hopefully you've preemptively answered most already. If people are asking stupid questions, that were clearly shown in the advert, I usually rule them out as tenants. They will be the demanding tenants that ask you to fix a lightbulb, then realise the bulb wasn't broken, they had just been using the wrong switch. You laugh, I cried, this happened to me once.

It can be hard to remember good tenants and bad tenants, especially when there are a lot of them. There is an easy way to covertly take notes. Print out an A4 Sheet with everyone's names on, and some columns with titles that only you know what they mean. For instance: 'Name' 'Attendance' 'Dates Confirmed' 'Times Confirmed'. This will mean nothing to the tenants, but you can use it to record good tenants and bad. For instance if you particularly like a group of tenants put a tick in the dates confirmed box, if you really don't like a group put a tick in times confirmed box. It's a secret cipher that only you know and will be really useful when you're comparing applications later.

Now let's get to the online application. To make your life easier, I've built a neat application tool which you can use on my website www.advancetogo.com/application There are lots of questions that you might like to ask people, to see if they are a good fit to rent your property. Here are a few of the basics: When do you want to move in? (If someone wants to move in two weeks after the property is available, you're going to lose half a month of rent... What is your employment? (Can they afford the rental...) Is it permanent or temporary? (What happens if they lose their job in 2 months time...) Who else will you be living with? (How many people will be in the property, will this increase the needed maintenance work...) How well do you know the other tenants? (Will people fall out and want to move out in a couple of months time...) Add in as many or as few questions as you need to help you choose.

There are a few questions that you must ask. "The rent is advertised at £XXXX, lots of tenants are interested, can you offer above the asking rental? What is the most you are comfortable paying?" The other important question is "How many months rent in advance are you able to pay?"

These may seem like capitalistic, intrusive and unfair questions but they are not. You must ask tenants these questions to find out exactly what the fair market price of your property is. You're not forcing tenants to rent from you, you're just asking them what's the most they are able to pay and you're ensuring that the situation is a competitive one where they are likely to put forward their best offer.

At this point in the rental process it's important to keep momentum up, you want things to happen fast and you have to strike while the iron is hot. You should tell tenants at the viewing that it will be possible to apply online through the link for the next four hours. After that you will select tenants within 24 hours. This lets everyone know that the process is going to happen fast, it creates urgency, it heightens the fear of missing out and it ensures that you do get the very best offer.

After the viewing, it's a good idea to review any notes that you took, or write down any particular tenants you like, or any that you didn't. It's best to do this straight after as you won't remember the details for long, in fact by the time you are reviewing the applications in four hours, you'll likely have forgotten any useful information that would help you pick the right tenants!

So you've had a coffee, gone to the gym, got your 10,000 steps and are now ready to review the applications. Brilliant. There are three different data sources that you need to use in making your decision. Your personal impressions from meeting the tenants, the information in the application forms and the meta-data. The meta-data are insights that you can gather from how tenants have responded. Who filled in the form first, how detailed were their answers. Were they too detailed?

I like to keep the application review process simple. There are only a few considerations that I take into account: who has offered to pay the most rent? Who has offered the most rental in advance? Who can move in first? Who would not make me cry, if I was stuck in an elevator with them for a day?

The main reason you've become a property investor is financial, you want to make money. Getting the best amount of rental per month is key, however many times over the years I have turned down the highest rental offers because I did not like the tenants. I would not have fun managing them during the tenancy. The character types I strongly avoid are the neurotic ones, the people who are going to complain too much and make your life difficult. You want to avoid them at all cost, even if it means taking a lower rental offer.

The next variable is 'rent in advance'. For those of you who want to grow a portfolio of properties this can help get your next deposit ready quickly. For instance one tenant group offers to pay you £2200 per month, but can only pay rent each month. Another tenant group offers to pay you £2100 a month, but can pay 10 months upfront at the start of the tenancy. This will give you £21,000 which is a serious lump of cash, and could be used as a deposit payment on your next buy to let property investment. Getting rent payments in advance saves you a lot of admin time checking and chasing rent payments. Having the rent in advance also tends to lead tenants to be less demanding, they've already paid and are generally happier tenants to get on with. They cannot withhold rent as a prelude to any communication or demand. Some authorities have a cap on how many months rent you can be paid in advance, make sure you are compliant before accepting advanced rental.

Void loss is another important consideration when choosing tenants. Let's make this comparison easier. You have two tenants groups who are the same in every way. They are both lovely and they both want to pay £2,200 per month. However one can move in on the first day the property is available, the other can't move in until two weeks later. That two week delay will leave your investment property empty for two weeks, making no rent. You'll lose £1015 in potential income while the property is vacant. This is called the 'void loss', in this example the decision is easy, make an extra £1,015 and take the tenants who can move in straight away.

In other examples, you might want to take pen and paper to work out exactly what the best financial outcome is for you. Perhaps one group has offered more monthly rental, but want to move in later and, overall, you're better to take the tenants who will move in straight away, but will pay less.

How much did you spend on your last city break away? Oh you went to a nice European city. Did you spend £500 a night on a five star hotel? I ask this because I don't want you to forget the value of money. Tenants offering to pay £83 a month more will make you an extra £1,000 over the year. This is a huge amount of money. You could spend it on an incredible city break in outrageous luxury. Don't sacrifice your income lightly. Perhaps one group is a tiny bit nicer than the other but they have offered less, you think you'd like to rent to them… would you pay for them to have a £1,000 luxury weekend away? Do you like them so much that you would give them that £1,000 gift? I didn't think so. Remember you're a patient investor who looks at time scales with a financial wisdom beyond your years. Little monthly sums will add up to a lot of money in the long term.

Once you've chosen tenants you need to lock in their commitment. The faster you complete a deal the less chance it has of falling through. The best way to do this is to get them to pay the security deposit. In the UK tenants can still pull out of the deal after they have paid the security deposit and are entitled to a full refund, so you also want to get them to sign the lease agreement as soon as possible. Once they have signed it's highly unlikely that the deal will fall through.

You may decide to use a tenant referencing agency to verify that the tenant has been truthful about their income, and that they don't have bad references or a history of missing rent payments. Tenants failing referencing is a potential reason why a rental deal could fall through after the lease has been signed.

Now you might think that you should send them the lease agreement first, as it's the legally binding commitment. You don't have to do that. It's easier to ask them to pay the deposit first. Although this doesn't legally bind the tenant, it emotionally binds them. I have never had a tenant pull out after paying the deposit.

Reading the lease agreement takes a lot of time. Tenants are likely to ask for changes, or to query parts that they don't understand. This gives them a window of time during which they might view another property and pull out.

Here is the worst case scenario. You choose a tenant group and then send them the lease. You tell all the other tenants that you've now let the property and you are sorry that you haven't picked them. 4 days and many phone calls and emails later, the tenants you chose have not yet signed the lease. They are still waiting for someone's mother's cousin's friend who is a lawyer to give their feedback on it. The tenant group has actually just looked around another property that they like more and they decide to pull out. Now you desperately email all of the other applicants but almost a week has gone by, some have found other properties while some just feel rejected and no longer want to rent from you. You've got to start the whole process of advertising again, and you've wasted a huge amount of time and energy. Don't do this!

Once the tenants have paid the deposit you then need to create a lease agreement. Most local councils have standard lease agreements that you can use for free and that are up to date with the latest legislation. When the lease agreement is created you can send it to be signed online. I use a great online signing service called 'sign now'. When it is signed and the deposit money has cleared you should give yourself a reward. Well done you've worked hard and you've accomplished something incredible. You've just let your first investment property to tenants and you're making your financial freedom happen!

In a perfect world your tenants would stay forever and every few years you'd increase the rent. Your tenants would be competent and would handle all maintenance. They would keep the property in good repair and you would never hear from them ever again. You'd just get a chunk of money in your bank every month, appearing like magic thanks to your foresight and hard work. You might be surprised but the reality can be pretty close to this. I had a three year lease to two marvellous students, and in the whole three years, I only had to deal with one maintenance issue, they paid their rent on time every month, never missing a single payment.

Having a good process for selecting tenants will help you achieve the best rental and the lowest management workload.

Being a Good Landlord

The tenant landlord relationship is stereotypically a negative one. Landlords worry that tenants won't pay rent and will wreck the property. Tenants worry that landlords will steal their deposits and be unresponsive to maintenance requests. It doesn't have to be this way. Moving home is stressful for tenants, the start of a tenancy gives you the opportunity to break the stereotype and show your tenants that you're a good landlord. Getting off on the right foot will make managing the property easier and it can increase how long tenants stay with you. It also doesn't take a lot of effort, just some thoughtfulness on your part.

The majority of problems in a tenancy are caused by unrealistic expectations, this is why it's so important to get started correctly. If you can, time and geography permitting, it's best to meet your tenant in person on their move-in day. I always like to welcome the tenant to their new home by giving them a present. My default is to put a bottle of wine in the fridge, a nice box of chocolates on the kitchen table, and some fresh flowers in the living-room or toilet. Instantly this little effort that will cost you no more than £20 will break the expected negative landlord tenant relationship. It will reset their assumptions and ingratiate you with them. It also activates the psychological rule of reciprocity, as you've given them something unexpected they will feel in your debt. Investing £20 here will hugely reduce your stress levels later if you have problems with your tenant. It also shows that you do care.

If you're able to meet your tenant in person, then I'd recommend giving them an in-depth guided tour of the house. Run through some of the simple things. Here is how you turn the heating on, here is how you set the hot water temperature. This is how you clean the filter on the washing machine, here is how you change the lightbulbs. Going through the most common questions and maintenance issues makes it clear to the tenant that you expect them to be proactive in handling these things. If they call you at 10pm on a Sunday evening, you're not going to go over to change a lightbulb.

Although it is time consuming, I highly... highly recommend you put all of this common sense information into a welcome pack / move in pack. Putting this together is an asset that will save you days' worth of time over the years that you have the property.

A good move-in pack should contain a 'how to' guide for running the home. Everything from where the bins and recycling need emptied, right through to setting up a new account for electricity and gas. Rather than writing a huge to-do list in this chapter I've put together an editable move-in pack on my website that you can download as a PDF, visit www.advancetogo.com/moveinpack

As a landlord, you take on a 'Duty of Care' for your tenants. This is something that you need to take very seriously. If your boiler malfunctions due to lack of maintenance, and carbon monoxide kills your tenant, you are responsible. You won't get a fine, or a slap on the wrist. You'll be convicted of manslaughter and sent to jail. That's how serious we're talking.

So it's essential to provide safety documentation and include it with the move-in pack. The annual safety certificates you should have are: a gas safety certificate for a boiler and or gas fire; a PAT test (portable appliance test) for electrical safety; a fire alarm system test, a fire inspection certificate that checks you've got a working fire extinguisher and fire blanket in the property. Every five years you should get an EICR (electrical installation condition report) that ensures all your wiring is safe.

Perhaps I've scared you, and you're worried about a tenant dying and your easy investment plan turning into a jail sentence. Let me talk you down a little… If you have got a valid gas safety certificate, and the boiler malfunctioned and the tenant died, then it would not be your fault. Either the engineer that provided the gas safety certificate, or the appliance manufacturer would be at fault, and they would be off to prison not you. So if you keep on top of your paperwork, you'll never put your tenants or yourself at any risk.

The next must-have document… It's the inventory report! If you've decided to rent the property furnished, or unfurnished, you still must have an inventory report. This is a document that details the condition of all fixtures & furniture: carpets, windows, chairs, everything. Being a landlord can make you just a tiny bit biased when it comes to reporting the condition of bits and bobs. While you might say the sofa is "as good as new", someone else might call it slightly worn. Getting an independent inventory clerk to create the inventory solves any bias problems.

A professional inventory should cost around £99. The clerk will list, photo and record the condition of all fixtures and fittings. In a perfect world the property is returned to you in good condition at the end of the tenancy. In reality this doesn't often happen. Which is why it's worth investing £99 in the inventory. If things are damaged you can pay the inventory clerk to do a check out and to provide an unbiased appraisal of any damage cost. Instead of you saying the tenant is liable to pay for repairs, the inventory clerk will do it, meaning you are not the bad guy. The tenant is more likely to pay in this situation as they are being told what to do by an unbiased arbitrator not a greedy landlord.

In my experience, the number one thing that pisses tenants off, is bad communication. I find that as a landlord you don't have to solve tenants problems immediately, but you do need to acknowledge them. You've done such a good job of showing the tenant around, explaining their responsibilities, setting their expectations and giving them a wonderful information pack that you're unlikely to get to many maintenance issues... In case you do, it's good to have a communication plan for how you expect tenants to contact you, and letting them know how you will respond.

The most effective solution that I've found is WhatsApp groups. All of my properties have more than one tenant. Setting up a WhatsApp group with myself and all of the tenants makes it really easy to communicate. It also means that everyone can see all of the messages.

As you've done a great job of treating the tenant with respect, and you've explained their responsibilities and made it easy for them to look after the property, you hope they won't wreck it. Another step you can take to make sure tenants look after your investment is to schedule proactive maintenance inspections.

At the start of the tenancy agree a date once per quarter where you will come to inspect the property. In the information pack there is a page that explains to the tenants how to clean the property and the standard of cleaning that is expected. Make sure you remind the tenants about this before the inspection so that they have the property clean for when you come round. Doing this means the property will be cleaned at least four times a year and increase the probability that tenants will leave the property clean at the end of the tenancy.

These inspections are a great chance for you to get proactive with maintenance. You're a long term investor meaning that you want to keep the property in rentable condition for as long as possible. If you don't do any maintenance work on the property then it will get so worn out that you won't be able to rent it, or you won't be able to rent it for a good price. Then you'll have to take the property off the market for a few weeks, or a few months to do the maintenance work. Managing maintenance reactively means you will miss out on rent payments, and your income will drop.

Leaving maintenance to the last minute is also much more expensive. A great example of this is windows. Make sure that the window frame, particularly the bottom part, is always in good condition. If you let the paint peel, the sealant crack, and the wood rot, then water will get in. This will mean that you have to replace the window frame and you'll likely have to re-plaster the damp wall and then repaint it. Messy, expensive and time consuming work. It's much faster and cheaper to simply make sure that the window frames are painted every few years.

There is a list of common maintenance jobs that you can cheaply do while the property is tenanted. Simple things like replacing silicone sealant in the shower, painting your windows and oiling locks. I've created a PDF inspection document that you can download on my website www.advancetogo.com/inspectiondocument.

Do consider furniture and fittings upgrades as an investment. Fair wear and tear will eventually degrade all of these, so plan to re-invest part of your income in keeping your property desirable.

In this chapter you've learned that extra effort and proactive maintenance will make a tenancy run smoothly. By being a good landlord you spend less time on management, get less stressed and make more money. It's a win-win situation for you and your tenants, congratulations!

Tenant & Landlord

Buying a house is a big decision, it is daunting. Most people don't think buying a property is accessible to them, and when they do think about buying, they think about buying a home to live in, not as a buy to let property investment.

There is a conceptual barrier to buying an investment property to let out. "How can I buy a property as an investment, if I don't even own my own home yet?" Most people think that while they are a tenant they can't also be a landlord.

News flash, it is okay to be both a landlord and a tenant. In fact it's okay to be a portfolio landlord with lots of rental properties and to still be a tenant. I am strongly in favour of being both a landlord and a tenant. There are practical and financial reasons for this.

Practically you might not want to be tied down to one geography. We have the opportunity to be more mobile than ever before and renting provides a lot of flexibility. When renting you can change location, property size, and rental budget with relative ease, your biggest commitment is usually a 12-month lease no more.

Financially it might be cheaper for you to rent than to own, this is the case if you can rent your desired home for less per month than your investment property makes. For instance you have the option to a) rent your home for £1000 per month, or buy it for £100,000. You also have the option b) to invest £100,000 in a buy to let investment property that makes £1,250 per month from letting the property out and you continue renting your current home for £1000 per month.

In this example it's a better decision to buy the investment property and to rent your own home as you'll make an extra £250 per month which adds up to a nice £3,000 per year. (This is assuming that both properties have the same capital appreciation.) You will also have the benefit of flexibility, it's easy for you to move. It's worth making this calculation to see if you are financially better off buying a place to live or buying an investment property. I've created a comparison calculator on my website www.advancetogo.com/calc so you can make an informed decision.

The point that I want to drive home; investing in a rental property is achievable and you should not put owning your own dream-home as a barrier to investing in property.

Start Today

Earning your financial freedom is going to take a lot of motivation and energy. You can break every barrier. If you don't have money readily available for a deposit it might take you years to save up but you will get there. Don't be scared of getting into debt. You've learned how to use the power of compound interest to your gain. Nothing can stop you from winning your financial freedom.

Now that you've learned how to succeed in property, you deserve a break. Have a little day dream. What will you do with an extra £1,000 a month spending money? Will you save it up for something special? How do you feel knowing that throughout your retirement you'll have extra rent money on top of your pension? How do you feel knowing you have a nest egg of hundreds of thousands of pounds in case of emergency or medical bills? Does it make you smile knowing you have wealth to give to your children when they start their families? Do you feel excited about those daydreams?

Brilliant, let's begin the work of turning your dreams into reality.

Printed in Poland
by Amazon Fulfillment
Poland Sp. z o.o., Wrocław

57286067R00069